Miracles Miracles Miracles

Signs and Wonders from the Worldwide, Whirlwind Ministry of Charles and Frances Hunter

by Charles Frances Hunter

Books By Charles and Frances Hunter

A Confession A Day Keeps The Devil Away
A Tribute to God
The Angel Book
Born Again! What Do You Mean?
Come Alive
Don't Be Afraid Of Fear
Feasting on Prosperity
Follow Me
Get Ready! Get Ready! Get Ready! to be Overtaken and Overcome by the Blessings of God
God Is Fabulous
God's Answer To Fat . . . LOØSE IT!
God's Big "IF"
God's Healing Promises
Revised Handbook For Healing
Healing Is For You
Hot Line To Heaven
How to Develop the Gifts of the Spirit
How To Develop Your Faith
How To Find God's Will
How Do You Treat My Son, Jesus?
How To Heal The Sick
How To Make Your Marriage Exciting
How To Pick A Perfect Husband . . . Or Wife
How To Receive And Maintain A Healing
How To Receive And Minister The Baptism With The Holy Spirit
How to Walk in Victory Every Day of Your Life
I Promise . . . Love, God
Impossible Miracles
Laugh Yourself Healthy
Let This Mind Be In You
Memorizing Made Easy
Scriptures to Live By
Shout The Word / Stop The Thief
Strength For Today
Supernatural Horizons
The Fabulous Skinnie Minnie Recipe Book
The Supernatural Spine
The Two Sides Of A Coin
There Are Two Kinds Of . . .
Watch Out! The Devil Wants Your Mind
What's In A Name?
What's New??

ISBN 1-878209-42-6   LARGE PRINT EDITION

Table of Contents

Miracles, Miracles, Miracles

Published by
HUNTER BOOKS
P. O. Box 5600 • Kingwood TX 77325
(281) 358-7575 • (281) 358-4130 Fax
Website: www.cfhunter.org
eMail: wec@cfhunter.org

Introduction

Too much of the Christian world has slept for two thousand years since Jesus gave the Great Commission and told us all to preach the gospel, cast out devils, minister the baptism with the Holy Spirit, and heal the sick. We are in the end times, and Jesus has much still to be done in the earth before He can return. This is the hour of the believer! God is calling every believer to come off of their comfortable, soft, padded pews and begin to be men and women who actually cause the words of Jesus to become a reality in today's world!

As its title proclaims, this is a book of miracles. But the exciting thing is, we are not only going to share what has happened to and through us, but we are going to share signs and wonders which have happened through others who have taken our *How to Heal the Sick* training and who are stepping out in faith and becoming believers of action!

God never intended for one or two specially selected disciples to go out and do the Great Commission. He gave that command to every single believer. For the last quarter of a century, God has put it in our hearts and souls to teach believers that "If Charles and Frances can do it, you can do it, too!" ...and also "If Jesus did it, you can do it, too!" In fact, you can do even greater things because Jesus said so in His word!" (John 14:12). This commission is the very core of our teaching. This is the breath of our lives.

During our Healing Explosions and through ongoing and current training with live healing schools, television, videos, DVDs, books and Internet, we have trained thousands and thousands of believers that, in the name of

Jesus and by the power of the Holy Spirit, every believer can accomplish signs, wonders and miracles today, in the twentieth century. *Jesus Christ is the same yesterday, today, and forever* (Hebrews 13:8). He has not changed, nor has the Great Commission changed one bit! Today believers are becoming real "doers" of the word. Wherever we have taken this message of the believer doing the Great Commission, it has spread like wildfire. There is revival going on all over the world!

As you read through our stories and the testimonies we have witnessed or have later received from people, you will see that "God is no respecter of persons." You will read how the miraculous occurred in the lives of young children, teenagers, and adults of all ages, people from every nation, every denomination and every walk of life.

It would be impossible for us to write about every sign and wonder which has followed us over the years, simply because there would not be enough room to contain the incredible accounts. It would also be impossible for us to print each and every letter of testimony which we have received since our teachings on *How to Heal the Sick* began circling the globe. We have selected some of our favorite signs and wonders plus a sampling of what has happened across the world through ordinary, everyday, miracle-working believers because they have been trained "how to heal the sick." Some of the stories we have selected happened years ago and some happened only a few days ago. God is still moving and so are his disciples!

Charles and Frances Hunter

Chapter 1

Supernatural Beginnings

I LOVE THE SUPERNATURAL! I guess one of the reasons is that I was born into the kingdom of God through a supernatural experience. As a result, I associate all things concerning God and Jesus Christ totally with the supernatural.

How well I remember the night God wiped all the printing off of the page of my Bible where Psalm 23 was written, and revealed a snow white page. Then He proceeded to write on it in the brilliant red blood of Jesus!

The words He wrote were life-changing: "Frances Gardner (that was my name then), I love you!" Five words were all that He wrote, but it was enough to make me realize for the first time in my life that God loved me personally as an individual, and not just as part of the "world" that He sent Jesus to redeem.

Charles' life was also totally changed through the supernatural. After thirty-one years as a leader in the church, he was completely transformed and baptized with the fire of the Holy Spirit by making a simple statement to God: "Take all of my life and make me spiritually what YOU want me to be!" He was transformed in the twinkling of an eye after all those years of trying to live a holy life!

It was only natural that our love affair should be supernatural. We met and married without ever having a date, or ever seeing each other from the time we met until we were married just eighty-eight days later. These complete stories are told in previous books, *God is Fabulous*, *Follow Me,* and *How to Pick a Perfect Husband...or Wife*.

With such supernatural events drawing us into God's plan, I suppose it was only natural that our walk with God would be totally in the supernatural! God had ordained from the very beginning that we should walk in the miraculous! Since we were over a hundred years between us when we got started, every year since then has been a whirlwind of the supernatural, as though God wanted to help us catch up to what we could have done had we started when we were much younger.

From the instant we received the baptism of the Holy Spirit the desire of our hearts has been to breathe a real and active discipleship into the lives of others. Jesus' command in Mark 16 is so burned in our hearts we can hardly think of anything else. It is as through God placed a red-hot brand on our hearts which contained the Great Commission of the Bible.

Go into all the world and preach the gospel to every creature. He who believes and is baptized will be saved; but he who does not believe will be condemned. And these signs will follow those who believe: In My name they will cast out demons; they will speak with new tongues; they will take up serpents, and if they drink anything deadly, it will by no means hurt them; they will lay hands on the sick, and they will recover. (Mark 16:15-18).

Although this scripture has been in the Bible all the time, it seems as though God has shined down a glorious light on it. It radiates and pulsates from our innermost being. We live it, we eat it, we sleep it, we love it, we think it, we speak it, and we do it at all times! Now with a combined age of 180, we are just as passionate every day as we were the day we trained our first believer to lay hands on the sick. We rejoice every single day that, all over the world, signs and wonders are still multiplying as the people of God come alive to the fact that each of us must be out there doing what Jesus told us to do.

Chapter 2

Living the Book of Acts

Luke, the Great Physician wrote the most exciting book of the Bible, and I believe the Holy Spirit chose Luke because a doctor really looks at the details. Acts is absolutely alive with the power of God, and what is so exciting is that it records everyday people getting baptized with the Holy Spirit, forgetting all their past and all their fears and going out doing the works that Jesus did! They didn't do it the same way all the time, they had challenges along the way, but they obeyed Jesus and created a legacy for every believer to follow until Jesus returns.

Do you know how many chapters are in the book of Acts? I suppose every Bible that would be found on this planet would show that Acts has 28 chapters. But I believe with all my heart and soul that Acts is still being written today, and when we read the Bible as it will appear in heaven, any of us who have obeyed what Jesus told us to do, will find our names in the hundredth or thousandth or millionth chapter of Acts!

Let's get started now and enjoy the excitement and thrill of God's miracle working power happening today, that we will undoubtedly read about in some of those ongoing chapters in the heavenly Bible.

We had attended a pastors' and leaders' meeting in Charlotte, N.C. where we met the pastor of an Assembly of God church in Ormond Beach, Florida. He invited us to come to his church on the one night still available in our Florida schedule and insisted he could put a good meeting together in four days. More than 1,000 people showed up to jam the church on a Monday night, with just those four days' notice!

After an incredible praise and worship service, we shared on the miraculous things God is doing today, and then we asked if there was anyone in the audience who had tremendous pain. We wanted only someone who was experiencing serious pain at that particular moment.

A Leap of Joy

Over on the right hand side of the church, a young woman lifted her hand. She was a Southern Baptist who had gone to the doctor that afternoon for her final check-up before surgery on Wednesday. On her way to the doctor, she had seen the sign in front of the church which said, "Miracle Service Tonight With Charles and Frances Hunter."

After she passed the sign, several thoughts went through her mind: "Could God really do it today? Does God still heal today? Would God heal me?" She did not realize the Holy Spirit was speaking to her. She pondered about some teaching she had previously received on whether God still heals today, but those Holy Spirit inspired thoughts would not leave her. She decided she had nothing to lose, and asked some friends to bring her to the church that night.

After she raised her hand, ushers assisted her up onto the stage because she was in such agony she could not walk by herself. Pain was obvious with every step she took and was reflected in her voice with every word she spoke. A chiropractor was in the audience, so we asked him to examine her. He reconfirmed the fact that she had an area of such intense spasm that it indicated a ruptured disc.

The Bible says in Romans 4:17 that we can call into being those things which do not exist as though they did exist, bringing faith into reality; so we sat her down in a chair and commanded a new disc to form in her back. Her legs were uneven due to the intense pull in her back. When the supernatural power of God went into her spine, her leg moved back into proper position. Before we even told her to get up, the girl jumped up from the chair and screamed, "It doesn't hurt anymore! It doesn't hurt anymore!" She began to run back and forth across the stage as the entire church stood and began to cheer and praise God!

The rostrum was raised three steps above the auditorium floor, so we suggested she walk up and down the three stairs to make real sure she was healed. She shocked the entire church, but probably alarmed the chiropractor most of all, as she slowly, deliberately walked to the back of the stage, step by step, and then turned and ran all the way across the stage and LEAPED out into the audience, landed on her feet and took off running. We were glad she was not an athletic broad jumper or she would have landed with a crushing thud on someone's lap. The audience received a shot of faith adrenalin as she took that leap and demonstrated her healing.

The chiropractor put his hands over his eyes and exclaimed, "Oh, no!" But she kept right on running with absolutely no pain. The chiropractor later told us, "If God hadn't healed her, she would have just exploded her back." Her back did not explode, but faith exploded in that church, and scores of miracles followed that one! When the girl went back to her doctor, he cancelled her scheduled surgery!

Black-Eyed Peas and Cornbread

After witnessing such a wild introduction to the miraculous, a man came forward who was eighty-two years of age and appeared to weigh not much more than eighty-two pounds. His bent and twisted body was in severe pain from arthritis.   Muscles had atrophied in his legs, arms and feet. He had also undergone surgery to remove his stomach and had not been able to eat for many months.

We ministered healing to the arthritis first by casting out the spirit of arthritis.   Then we commanded a brand new stomach to form in his body by the power of the Holy Sprit and all pain to leave in the name of Jesus.

Suddenly this old gentleman who had hobbled up to the stage realized that all of his pain was gone and his body could do exactly what he wanted it to, and he began to dance all over the stage. He leaned this way and stretched that way and tested his body all over the place with absolutely no pain. He was so excited that he said he was going to go right home and fill up that new stomach with black-eyed peas, cornbread and buttermilk. Hallelujah! We were back in that area a month later, and his friends reported that was exactly what he did – gorged himself on black-eyed peas, cornbread and buttermilk and had no problem eating anything and everything else that he wanted!

From Looking Gray to Feeling Great

It is amazing how the power of God escalates and faith explodes when there are a few visible miracles. This church which had only a few days of anticipation experienced a night of great rejoicing as all kinds of diseases were healed.

A man who was dying of cancer could hardly walk to the platform. He was in excruciating pain and had a horrible death-like gray cast to his skin. We commanded the foul spirit of cancer to come out in the name of Jesus, commanded all the root and seed of cancer cells to die, and commanded the marrow of his bones to manufacture healthy, red blood.

The church watched breathlessly as the ashen pallor faded and healthy color returned to his face. Then he noticed that his pain had completely disappeared. This elderly saint who had dragged himself up to the front walked away rejoicing in the Lord, his face beaming and his cane waving in the air!

Can you imagine the impact of the life-changing miracles each of these people experienced? If Charles and I had stayed on our church pew, we would never have witnessed what God wants to do every single day. Signs and wonders will follow the believer, if we will just get out there and fulfill the Great Commission!

Chapter 3

Camp Meeting Time

God takes us into interesting and unusual places to do interesting and unusual miracles. Such was a time when we ministered in a large Dallas, Texas, camp meeting under a tent on a sweltering July 5th evening. There are times that God "shows off" for television, and this was one of those exciting demonstrations of his power.

We called for people who had severe pain in their body, because those are always the easiest to really know they have been healed. One of the first to come was a lady whose rib was so separated from the rest that you could put three fingers between two of her ribs. We commanded her arms to grow out and ribs to go back into place, in Jesus' name, and commanded the muscles, nerve, ligaments and tendons to be healed. What an impartation of faith went into the crowd when she immediately felt her ribs move into place and all pain leave!

As the people continued to come for ministry and depart from the stage totally healed, a man who had been observing finally made his way to the front. Wayne was the last one in line, and as he told his story, we could hardly wait to see what God was going to do.

He was a Vietnam veteran who, twenty years earlier, was hunkered down in a bunker when an 88 mm mortar shell made a direct hit. He was so seriously wounded that he required extensive surgery, but the highly trained surgeons were unable to remove all the shrapnel from his body. He required months in the hospital, during which time the shrapnel in his right leg deteriorated his hip joint, so a plastic hip joint was implanted. However, even after months of healing and rehabilitation, he could not bear his full weight on the implanted joint. He had also been "wired together" near the broken hip joint. Three discs in his spine were rubbing "bone on bone". His pain over the years had been severe and unrelenting.

To make Wayne's misery even worse, several years later, he suffered further injuries in a truck accident and was hospitalized for a month while he recovered from having his left side crushed. His left shoulder blade had been fractured like a broken dish. When he came to the stage, we could put a finger into the indentation where there should have been a solid section of shoulder blade.

We were confident in the power of God, so when he was examined by our chiropractors to verify all of his problems, we exclaimed, "That's easy!"

We commanded his leg to grow out and commanded the hip joint to be restored in Jesus' name. Then we laid hands on the broken shoulder blade and commanded all the bones to come together! We paused and watched breathlessly as God demonstrated a surge of his glorious power which we saw reflected in Wayne's surprised face.

We told Wayne, "Lift your arm!" To his amazement, his arm dramatically shot straight up! This was the first time he had been able to lift his arm more than half way. The audience went wild with excitement because the compassion of a crowd is always great towards a war veteran. He moved his arm around in every direction, including all the way around to touch the middle of his back. He said his wife had been washing his back since the truck accident, because his arm would not reach there.

Then we told him, "Test the rest of your body and see what God has done!"

He asked for a chair, sat down and began crossing his right leg over his left, time and time again. He broke into laughter and told the crowd, "There's not an artificial hip joint made in America that can do that! I haven't been able to do that since 1968!"

His joy was so contagious everyone was laughing and praising God right along with him. It is amazing how little things like crossing your legs become really important when you can't do them!

We then asked him to run down the ramp and into the audience. He looked at us with a quizzical expression, then took off running and laughing. We ran down the ramp behind him to meet him when he came back, and then directed him, "Let's see you run back up the ramp!"

He answered, "My wife can tell you that I can't even walk up a ramp like that." She came to his side and explained that he really could not walk uphill. She also testified that she had been healed two nights previously of arthritis.

Our response was, "Let's see which of you can outrun the other!" They dashed off together, but he was at the top when she was only half way there.

The stage was about eighteen inches higher than the ramp, and he put his left leg up on the stage and lifted his entire 185 pounds of weight. He stepped on and off the stage and did this over and over again. He could hardly believe his hip was working so perfectly. There was no pain left, his legs and arms were working perfectly, and the hip joint seemed like a brand new one.

We called Wayne a few days later, asking him how he was doing. He said that before his healing when he went up the stairs in his home, he had to pull himself up with his arms and almost drag the leg. But NOW he could run effortlessly up the stairs two steps at a time without hindrance or pain. His arm also was perfect.

As is our custom, we asked him to have his doctor x-ray his body, examine it, and give us a medical report, at our expense. He sent us a copy of the x-rays.

Shortly afterward, we were with a chiropractor and a medical doctor and asked them to take a look at the x-rays Wayne had sent. When they examined the x-rays, they both exclaimed, "Look at that shoulder blade! There's not even a hairline break there. Look at that hip socket!" They pointed out that the artificial hip joint was still there but God had grown human cartilage over the joint, so that it would function as normally as the joint he had been born with.

God can do His miracles any way he wants, and that is just fine with this happy Vietnam veteran, because he has absolutely no problems walking, leaping and praising God since he received his miracles! Hallelujah!

Chapter 4

A Healer Gets Healed – Plus a Bonus

Dr. Jim Hayes was a general practitioner near St. Augustine, Florida. He was the medical doctor who had been assisting us on the stage during the St. Augustine healing service. After he witnessed so many people receiving miracles, he asked if he could possibly be healed. And, of course, you know what we said!

He told us he had fallen from a second story building at the age of four. The fall had impacted his spine, and as a result he had lower back spasms and chronic pain. He then said that, for the past year, he had been unable to lift anything, to walk quickly or to even bend over without experiencing severe spasm and pain. He had been under the care of an orthopedic surgeon and an osteopath for about six months with some improvement, but was still limited by pain and stiffness.

When we ministered to him, he went away thanking Jesus, but we all really rejoiced when we received the following letter from him several months later:

"When you laid hands on me and grew out my right leg and commanded my pelvis to rotate and my back to be normal in the name of Jesus, I was instantly healed!

"As you remember, I immediately bent over and touched my toes with my knees unbent – something I never was able to do. I have been sharing this miracle with my patients and friends ever since, and I have been able to do all the things I couldn't do for years without pain. Praise God!

"I became a Christian during my first year of college about sixteen years ago at the age of seventeen. After graduating from medical school, I received the baptism with the Holy Spirit eight years ago and came to the realization that miracles and healing had not passed away as I had been taught.

"When we were first married in 1977, Barbara and I dedicated our future children to the Lord. We believed He would give us children in His perfect time. After five years of seeking Him and trusting Him but still not having any children, we sought medical help. We underwent many tests and procedures and were finally told our situation was hopeless. Every time I sought Him, He would tell me we *would* have children but would never say when.

"The healing of my back was so inspiring to us that we watched your video course, *How to Heal the Sick*. We heard you share that there were many 'Hunter babies' in the world and I realized God was leading us to have you pray for us in Jacksonville.

"As you recall, on Valentine's Day, after the doctors' panel in Jacksonville, Barbara and I asked for prayer to be healed of infertility after eight years of marriage. The Lord spoke through you, Frances, and said Barbara would conceive and deliver within one year. We both fell out under the power simultaneously. I knew God had finally answered our prayers. Barbara became pregnant within a month! Hallelujah!

"Since the Healing Explosion in Jacksonville, my ministry has literally exploded and I have been leading many patients to accept Jesus as their personal Lord and Savior. Some have been healed and baptized in the Holy Spirit as well.

"Jesus surely is the GREAT PHYSICIAN.

Love, Jim and Barbara"

I will never forget the day Jim called to let us know Barbara was pregnant. He didn't even have to use the telephone – I could have heard him all the way from Florida to Texas. And again when their little boy Joshua was born, his joy could not be contained!

Nothing is ever dull when you're walking in the supernatural with God! And the greatest joy is that so many of the people who receive a miracle in their own life, pass the love and power of God along to others. This is the Great Commission in action!

Chapter 5

Raise the Dead!

We were in a Mennonite church in a very small Pennsylvania town when I had a tremendous word of knowledge about a severe heart problem being healed. God spoke very clearly and said He was giving someone a new heart, so I asked if there was anyone there who had an extremely serious heart problem. It was difficult to understand the response because, where I had anticipated one person, more than twenty people came forward.

This never bothers me because I know in my spirit that God has a whole warehouse of spare parts. General Motors, as well as all other manufacturers, make spare parts for their products; and God is much smarter than all of the business geniuses in the world, so I know that He can give you a brand new part. As a matter of fact, Charles often says I have more new parts than originals.

We went down the line laying hands on everyone and speaking a creative miracle of a new heart into each of them. Everyone in the line fell under the power of God except one man. He looked quizzically around at me as if to say, "Why didn't I fall down?" and I said, "Don't worry, that's all right, you got a new heart!"

They all went back to their seats, and we continued the service. Suddenly I noticed a lot of activity around this man who had not gone down under the power. We tried to not allow this commotion to interrupt the service, but then we saw someone run out of the church and return with an oxygen tank. About this time, I decided I had better get down there. I walked up to the man and declared, "Brother, I didn't lay hands on you for a heart attack; I laid hands on you for a new heart!"

He immediately fell forward and gasped, "Nitroglycerine, nitroglycerine!"

Someone placed a nitroglycerine tablet under his tongue, and his son turned anxiously to me and relayed, "He has emphysema and diabetes as well."

I laid hands on him and commanded a new pancreas and new lungs in the name of Jesus! By this time, Charles came down off the stage to join me. After looking at him, we decided we should get an ambulance, so the church secretary ran to call one.

We asked the entire audience to get on their knees and pray, because we knew a man's life was at stake. Immediately, all of them began to pray fervently. One of the things we did not know was that this town was so small it did not have a hospital, or a doctor, or a paramedic, so they had to call a volunteer group about thirty minutes away.

We prayed and prayed, and sometimes I wondered if I was praying like the rest of them, because I was asking God to get that ambulance there in a hurry and get the poor man out of the church. I certainly didn't want him dying in a miracle service!

After what seemed an interminable length of time, the paramedics finally arrived. I felt we could breathe a little easier because when they rushed in, it was like a "D-Day" invasion! Seven of them ran to the man, began giving him oxygen and doing various other things. Suddenly everyone in the church heard them say on their portable phone, "Patient unstable! We don't know when we can move him!"

Do you have any idea how the heart of an evangelist beats when you have a critical situation like that on your hands? I thought, "Oh, no!"

Then the entire congregation doubled up on their prayers, because there is no way you can continue a service when there is a situation like that capturing everyone's attention.

The following is Charles' account of what he saw during those tense moments:

"I have seen the spirits of two different people when they left their bodies in death. I was watching the paramedics frantically working on the man, and at a point when it seemed they were especially alarmed, I saw the man's spirit leave his body like a vapor. It went up until it was half in the body and half above the body, moving upward.

"I said, 'Spirit of life, go back into him in the name of Jesus!' His spirit went back, but no sooner had it re-entered than up it came again, this time going completely above the body. I felt like trying to push it back in with my hands, but I knew the only power which could do this, so again I said, 'In the name of Jesus, spirit of life, go back into him!'

"Again it went back into the body. This was repeated seven times; and the seventh time, it stayed in his body. This was apparently the exact time the paramedics found him stabilized enough to take him to the ambulance and on to the hospital."

These twelve Jesus sent out and commanded them, saying:...Heal the sick, cleanse the lepers, RAISE THE DEAD, cast out demons. Freely you have received, freely give (Matthew 10:5, 8).

We breathed a deep sigh of relief.

Then what do you do after that? It was now quite late, and yet we knew there were many people who had come for a healing, so we announced, "If any of you would like for us to lay hands on you, we'll be glad to right now if you'll come forward."

We had the shortest healing line we have ever experienced in the history of our ministry! We never saw so many people go out the door as fast as they did! I'm not sure I blame them. We laid hands on the few who were left from that huge church, and then went to bed.

The town is so small that there was no motel or hotel, so we stayed in a room in the church. About midnight, there was a knock on the door. It was the pastor. With him was the son of the man who had the heart attack.

The young man said, "My father told me not to go home tonight until I had personally delivered a message to you. He said for me to tell you that he still has faith to believe he received a new heart!"

Even at that late hour, I was so excited that I screamed, "He got it, he got it!" After going through what he had just experienced, if he still had faith to believe he had a new heart, then I knew that the devil had not been able to rob him of what God had given him.

The pastor continued and told me that the man had been in a Baltimore hospital waiting for a quadruple by-pass for several months. Finally, an opening had come, but because they did not feel he could live through it, the doctors told him to come home and make arrangements for his funeral. The pastor heard the news and went over and invited him to the miracle service, telling him he believed he could be healed! Instead, he had a massive heart attack!

My spirit leaped within me even at this news, because I knew that the man had not lost his faith! It is at times like this that the devil loves to come in and rob us of anything and everything God wants us to have, but that man absolutely did not listen to anything the devil had to say.

The local doctors called for a heart specialist because they knew he could not be moved to Baltimore. They took x-rays early the next morning. Then they took another series of x-rays because they could not believe what they saw! Instead of the old worn-out heart that needed a quadruple by-pass, they said they saw the heart of a "twenty-five-year-old athlete!"

Doctors kept him in the hospital for additional tests and, after five days, reported that they could find no trace of diabetes in his body, even though he had been using insulin for thirty-seven years! They checked his lungs for emphysema and found not a trace left!

They had no choice but to release him with x-ray proof that he had a new heart, new pancreas and new lungs! The following Sunday, he was back at the same church dancing in the Spirit on the stage with the pastor and sharing his testimony of what the Lord had done for him. The next year, this man was the star player on the church softball team! Glory to God, nothing is impossible with God, if we can just believe!

One Sign Follows Another

Several years later, a gentleman came to a Chattanooga miracle service dying from heart failure. The pastor of the church whispered to us at the beginning of the service that this was a very sick man, so we called him up quickly, laid hands on him, and he fell out under the power of God.

The worship and praise continued, but my spirit was not satisfied because I felt the miracle had not yet been completed; so at the conclusion of the worship service, we called him forward again. He then mentioned to us that he also suffered from severe diabetes and emphysema. That triggered in my memory the miracle story of the man who had received a new heart, pancreas and lungs in that tiny Pennsylvania town three years earlier.

As the man stood before us the second time, I related to him the entire miraculous story. God had a special purpose in reminding me of the other miracle so it could build his faith. His blood pressure was 250/114 when he was last seen by the doctor who had told his wife that his heart had enlarged to eighteen centimeters across and was leaking blood. The doctor had told them that it was too late for a transplant. He and his wife realized that without divine intervention, his future in this earth was to be very short.

We laid hands on him again and spoke a new heart, pancreas and lungs into his body. When he fell under the power of God the second time, he suddenly realized that he could breathe deeply and had no pain in his chest whatsoever. When he went to his doctor's office the next day, the doctor turned pale and almost fainted as he asked him, "What happened to you?"

He simply replied, "God healed me."

Tests revealed his blood pressure was 127/82. The doctor heard a strong heart-beat, and x-rays showed the heart had reduced in size to normal and his lungs had cleared! He resumed working full time at his job, and he and his wife began having weekly *How to Heal the Sick* video schools in their home! A letter from his doctor is in our files. It is as follows:

"I am writing you at the request of one of my patients, who in my opinion experienced a 'miracle' in that he was literally at death's door and following this event at church, the state of his health was improved to an extent that was unexplainable by the laws of modern medicine.

"When he was initially seen by me, his congestive heart failure was as severe as any patient I have seen in twenty years and nothing short of a heart transplant would have kept him alive. I explained this moribund state to my patient and his wife and offered to refer him to one of the University Medical Centers, but he declined and told me at that time that he would leave his living or dying up to the Lord.

"My response was that the Lord must have had reasons unknown to us all for keeping him alive and that I would do all that I knew to do and leave it up to the Lord as to whether he lived or died.

"He will return to work next week and without a doubt could never have survived his heart failure without the Lord's intervention. It was indeed an act of God."

One sign and wonder follows another. That is why we encourage people to do what the Bible tells us, "Tell often what the Lord has done for you!" (Mark 5:19). In sharing the miracle of one man, another man got healed of exactly the same problems and then passed on his blessing of God by training others. The fact that miracles follow after us is good enough reason for you to believe they can follow after you as well!

Chapter 6

Let's Go to a Healing Explosion!

The world is fed up with dead religion. They want to see a living Jesus! They are tired of being powerless – they want the supernatural power of God in their lives!

We had seen our first miracles in tiny meetings in homes, churches, school buildings, and gradually larger churches and auditoriums across the country. It soon became apparent that God had much more on His mind than ministering to a few dozen or a few hundred thirsty believers, and it was pounding in our hearts to teach every disciple to get on fire with the Great Commission and go into all the world with signs and wonders following. We videotaped our 14-hour teaching series, *How to Heal the Sick*, showing actual miracles and methods of ministering to specific needs, and made it available to church leaders and believers.

The *How to Heal the Sick* videotapes (now also on DVD) and accompanying books became a current of living water which grew into streams and then rivers across the nation and into all the world. Believers got the message! Healing teams were eagerly meeting to watch the videotapes and then "practice" on each other. They were seeing signs and wonders in their midst long before they even got to minister in the Healing Explosions.

Minneapolis was not our first Healing Explosion, and no explosion was "typical". Each had its own unique flavor, but I want to take you to Minneapolis as an example which will bring you into the flow of electrifying power and anointing of God that accompanied each one of these spiritually historical events.

Exciting Preparations

So you won't miss a single thing, let's start at the very beginning with the advanced training sessions which are really life-changing to every person who attends them.

The Minneapolis healing teams, totaling approximately 2,000 trained believers, were ready for the glory of God to fall on them, plus anything else and everything else God had in mind! The praise started off on an extremely high plane. Praise and worship is so vital because it is the plow that makes the furrow to open hearts so people can receive God's blessings. The glory of God filled the atmosphere, and then came a spine-tingling message from the Lord through Charles:

"I the Lord God have gathered into this room this night a very, very peculiar people. There has never, in all of My creation on earth, there has never been this number brought together who were trained and ready to go out to do My work supernaturally.

"Never before upon this earth until this night has there been such a group of this type. I see you. I know each little mark upon your body. I know your hearts. I know your thoughts. I know your desires. I know why you are here. I know how I brought each of you together and ministered My Spirit upon you till I brought you to this point, but I, the Lord God, say to you now, this is merely the beginning of your life.

"Just as great to Me," saith the Lord God, "as when I formed Adam and made him not afraid and saw a living being that was mighty and powerful, a brilliant likeness of My own likeness...even this night, you know that I have created a group of people to be the body of My Son and you are a great host of those people, and this is just the beginning. Your life will multiply," saith God. "Each of you will multiply rapidly as you minister to others and they catch the vision...

"I have created as though it were a new reproductive system, so, as Adam and Eve could reproduce another, so it is that I have created you for that divine purpose of rapidly increasing and populating the earth with those in the likeness of you.

"Those who will do My work will create a great and mighty host all over this earth until My glory in people will cover the earth as the water covers the sea. So saith the Lord your God."

Praise Sends Power Over the City

When the presence and power of God becomes evident through praise and worship, and Christians are in one accord, then a series of wonderful things can begin to happen.

A pastor came running to the platform and shared the following exciting vision which brought the more than 2,000 trainees to their feet with wild excitement:

"As we began to worship tonight, I saw in the Spirit the worship go up and it was as though it went right through all of the floors and to the top of the hotel. It culminated there in the heavenlies and then like it had a command from God, it started marching as an army to the Met Center (site of the Healing Explosion). As the praise went forth, it was doing battle. There were a lot of powers of darkness, there was a lot of spiritual wickedness that it had to cut through, but as we continued, it kept rising up and the continued praise kept following. As it got to the Met Center, there were angelic beings. It was the warring angel standing over the Met Center.

"That warring angel began to give direction to the praise and he began to direct it around the Met Center into various seats in the auditorium, on the floor, all around the corridors. As it appeared to me, it was like there was a spiritual cleansing of that place. As the praise continued, there was still praise coming out of here, still going over there. It was like there was such an abundance that the warring angel began to direct the praise out in various directions all over the Twin Cities."

No More Baby Food for God's Army

With every breath of praise and worship, with every utterance prompted by the Holy Spirit, God's presence increased in intensity. The group assembled for the advanced training sessions was about ready to explode. Then the Holy Spirit gave me a most unique word from the Lord:

"For the last few years you have been like a baby on a bottle. You have been eating diluted food. But, He says, "I give it to you straight. No longer will your bottle be diluted with water. You will get it straight," saith the Lord. "No longer will you have to be on baby food which has been chewed up before it got to you. You will be able to take the strongest meat and to dissect it with your teeth.

"But," God says, "I am not sending out a powerless army. I'm not sending out an army that has been diluted, an army that has been watered down. I am sending out an army that is straight from the word GO and making him who has never even dreamed about being in a ministry have a ministry birthed tomorrow night at the Healing Explosion.

"I am sending you out to feed people instead of sitting there with a bottle in your mouth just drinking in, drinking in, drinking in," says the Lord.

"Now you go forth in the name of Jesus. Rays are going on to the churches that are continuing on, to the churches which are going to be making supernatural house calls, but these rays of praise will by-pass all of the churches which are going to still sit in a rut and are saying, 'That's too way out for me, I don't want to get involved.' Those rays of praise will go right straight to the churches which catch the vision."

It was difficult to come back into the natural after such an incredible succession of Holy Spirit ministry. Even after final instructions for the Healing Explosion were given, people did not want to leave God's presence. Gradually, the ballroom emptied, and a holy silence blanketed the room.

The Explosion!

June 6, 1986 was an "explosive" evening for the Minneapolis, Minnesota area. The Bloomington Met Center, usually used for such noisy sporting events as the Minnesota North Stars hockey team, was invaded by a totally different crowd. Prepared and trained to heal the sick, over 2,000 enthusiastic and turned-on healing team members took their places. Volunteers greeted the masses and directed traffic as the crowd pushed their way into the large auditorium to find their seats. As the parking lot filled with cars, campers and busses from hundreds of miles around, thousands more waited patiently outside to enter the arena. On and on they came – people hungering for what God had to offer during the great Minneapolis Healing Explosion.

The crowd was so receptive to the music that high praise and worship was reached within minutes of the start of the meeting. No one entered the building without feeling the power of God rush over them. Stepping into the actual arena was equally as awesome – a special "Holy Ghost glow" radiated from more than 11,000 believers singing God's praises.

After several special and powerful words from the Lord, we gave a call for salvation and the baptism with the Holy Spirit. As the crowd cheered and clapped, approximately 5,000 people stood and streamed down to the arena floor to receive the baptism with the Holy Spirit. It was electrifying because one of the most heart-thumping times in the Healing Explosions is to see the people respond when that call is made. As the people came down from the stands, it looked like streams of molten lava pouring down each stairway onto the great arena floor. Pastors wept with joy as the entire arena floor filled with spiritually hungry people!

Quite like the cheering that frequented this busy sports arena on many other evenings, the roar was deafening! However, on this very special occasion, the one that was honored was Jesus – the Hero, the Victor, the Healer!

Charles ministered the baptism, and under his instruction, they spoke in tongues, they sang in tongues, they whispered in tongues. And the power of God covered each and every one of them while photographers and cameramen from the local newspapers and TV stations scurried around shooting pictures of this momentous event in the Minneapolis area.

The crowd in the stands cheered, prayed and wept as they witnessed such a mighty move of God among the body of Christ. No one had ever seen anything like this in America before!

Armed and Ready for Action!

The healing teams were on fire and were prepared to devastate the devil's work. They had been strategically placed throughout the whole arena, interspersed between others who had come for healing. At a given signal, the teams were released to march into place, in a powerful procession all the way from the balconies, down the steps onto the arena floor, as vocalist Karen Wheaton led the crowd in a stirring "Battle Hymn of the Republic." The entire audience rose to their feet singing, "Mine eyes have seen the glory of the coming of the Lord; His truth is marching on," as the healing teams flowed in streams of faith and power onto the arena floor.

The magnitude of what God was going to do in Minneapolis became vividly evident as the 2,000-plus team members took their places on the floor as well as throughout the wheelchair sections. Wherever you looked, you could see the army of God dressed in full armor and prepared to set His people free.

Then, on cue from the platform, those who came for healing followed the teams onto the floor, and the teams were released to go to work! All the hours of training and study were put to good use as they began to minister to the thousands who had come expecting a miracle from God. Truly 2,000 new miracle-working disciples were beginning a new dimension as witnesses for Jesus.

We watched intently as the sick and hurting and terminally ill made their way over to waiting healing teams and received ministry from ordinary believers, just as Jesus said was His perfect will to be done in the earth. A hum of confident ministering voices composed an electrifying faith symphony which surely reached the ears of God.

For too long, many have felt that only the "stars" – the evangelists, the apostles, the prophets – could do the healing, and yet before our eyes we witnessed miracles and healings taking place through the obedience of people like Tom and Abby and Stephanie and Jim and Darla - ordinary people who were not content sitting on their church pews. Every day of our lives we praise God that He commissioned us to teach believers that "If Charles and Frances can do it, you can do it, too!"

How do you interrupt a service where God is moving all over the place? You watch and wait, you thrill to the beat of God's victory songs, and you anticipate hearing every single testimony, although you know it won't be possible to hear them all. When the Holy Spirit gives you that cue that it's alright to interrupt, you call the people to come and testify, and scores rush to the front, anxious to report their miracles. You ask trained ushers to begin screening the testimonies of those who line up in long queues chomping at the bit to tell their good news. Only a few will get to speak compared to the growing numbers in the lines, so the ushers choose those whose testimonies have been tested as much as possible and which will be exciting and faith-building to others.

The miracles are reported, healings are demonstrated on stage, and encouragement is given for them to go and have everything checked by their doctor and then write or call the ministry with their praise reports. The awe of God's Holy presence lingers even as the evening comes to a close and the crowd slowly, a few at a time, exits a building made by human hands but which contained, for a divinely appointed time, the power, the presence, the excitement and the glory of God's supernatural Healing Explosion.

The Proof of the Pudding is in the Eating

The testimonies on stage and the next morning at the Victory Breakfast are always the "proof of the pudding" that God has called believers to walk in the supernatural. When these exciting reports are shared, plus others which are later communicated by phone calls or letters, it makes our spirits soar!

Jesus Healed Me!

A little boy with cerebral palsy came up on the stage after healing team members laid hands on him. He was about four years old, and he kept opening and shutting his fist as he repeated over and over again, "I had cerebral palsy and I couldn't straighten my arm, and I couldn't open my hand, but Jesus healed me, and now I can!" He wanted everyone in the auditorium to know what Jesus had done for him; and little as he was, he gave all the credit to Jesus!

Hearing Without Ears

A little boy was there who had no physical ears, not even an opening where the ear should have been. Healing teams ministered to him, and when he came up on the stage, he was hearing perfectly. The ears had not formed yet, but they had started, and what was so exciting was that the hearing was already there! His face reflected pure amazement as he repeated words softly spoken to him behind his back. He could hardly contain his excitement, and joyful tears rolled down his little face!

Miraculous Speech, Hearing, and No More Glasses

A young lady came up onto the stage holding two hearing aids. When she was a little girl about one year old, a light bulb had exploded inside her mouth. Her ear drums were utterly destroyed, but she could hear slightly with very strong hearing aids. Her jaws were wired together, and she had no lips. The faith-filled healing team commanded reconstructive miracles to her inner ear, nerve system and bones. After being slain in the Spirit, she could hear a whisper and could speak without restriction. She didn't even realize she wasn't wearing her glasses! God really did a supernatural job on her – not through us, but through the healing team members who had been trained and were bold enough to believe God could do miracles!

Failure Becomes Victory

A woman came up who had arthritis in her back. The healing teams did everything they could think of, but nothing seemed to work. Finally they discovered she woman had unforgiveness in her heart towards someone who had deeply hurt her. We have learned that an unforgiving spirit can keep a lot of people from being healed. As soon as she got rid of the unforgiveness, she was completely healed. As she testified on the stage, her face radiated with joy as she realized that not only had the unforgiveness brought on the arthritis, but it had always kept her in bitterness, and now she was set free!

The testimonies don't end with the Healing Explosion, nor do they end with the Victory Breakfast. Truthfully, they should never end as we continue to do the things Jesus commanded us to do. The following letter will show how the very life of Jesus can operate in every believer – which is the true goal of the Healing Explosions:

The Gift Goes On

"I feel like a little kid coming home with a good report card for my mother to look at. So many opportunities have presented themselves just since yesterday after the Victory Breakfast.

"I am the woman who had the broken wrist who gave the testimony at the Victory Breakfast about hearing my wrist snap into place Thursday afternoon when we were practicing the 'neck thing' on each other. I wondered and was mystified by why God gave me such a wonderful experience. I thought it was maybe so I could tell my doctor; then I thought it was so I could tell my relatives and the people at church. But it's bigger than that. It is so I can tell *anyone* who asks me what happened to my wrist. God knows I'm bold enough to tell anyone! How could you keep still?

"In thinking about it, I think the wrist was actually dislocated as well as broken, and what I heard was it snapping back into place. We'll see when I go back to the doctor for my next visit, but just to let you know I'm in good shape, I'm typing this letter with full freedom of movement.

"The first thing I did Saturday afternoon was tell my neighbors who are staunch, fundamentalist, RLDS people (I live in an RLDS community of fifty families) who believe that only ordained priesthood members can administer to the sick with oil. I showed them the references in the Bible, the Book of Mormon and the Doctrine and Covenants which all agree on it. There was nothing they could say.

"Then I went to the grocery store and told the store manager and his wife and two other people standing nearby about the experience.

"As I walked away, a little lady trailed after me and said she only got part of it because she had been on a nearby telephone. I tried to pass over it quickly and get on with shopping but she said, 'Well, I have a lot of things wrong that I would certainly like to get healed of.'

"My ears perked up and I said, 'You would?'

"She said, 'Yes.'

"Can you guess what I said with a gleeful grin spreading across my face? I said, 'Do you want me to pray for you?'

"She said, 'Yes,'

"So I said, 'Well, come on. Let's find a place.' I took her in the manager's office, shut the door and started from the top down. When I finished, I said, 'Now, listen, Peggy. God's miracles will stand up under a microscope. So you don't have to have any fear when you go back to see your doctor.' Then I went about my business. Praise God! I can't imagine having this crazy boldness and the joy that comes with it.

"Since then, this cast was an opening for me to tell the story two more times that same afternoon. Once again today after church to a total stranger who was a guest and again Sunday night at 10:30 to a friend who needed prayer. It amazes me how the opportunities just present themselves right and left."

And a Little Child Shall Lead Them

The next letter touches my heart in a special way because, although the miracle is exciting, just as exciting is the fact that a little 9-year-old boy was one of the healing team members and he used his faith to minister healing to a perfect stranger. Just think what an impact that event has had on his life! The letter we received follows:

"When I was 22, after a slip on the ice, a trip to a chiropractor and x-rays, it was found that my back had never formed correctly. The last five bones in the spine formed almost an 'L' going off to the right. From the time of that slip on the ice, I had constant pain and occasional muscle spasms that went from my hip down to my ankle on the left side, as the muscles would try to pull the bones back into their correct position. Standing for any length of time was not pleasant as I constantly shifted from foot to foot to become comfortable. I was given back exercises by the chiropractor, which helped somewhat but I always had some pain.

"At the Healing Explosion, I went forward to be prayed with by a team consisting of a woman and her nine-year-old son. When they sat me down and prayed with me, I could feel and see my leg grow nearly an inch! I have had to readjust car mirrors for driving, my shoes no longer are worn down because I walk and stand perfectly comfortably, and I have had no back pain whatever since God's healing!"

The Angels Were There in Great Numbers

Do you remember at the beginning of this chapter, prior to the Healing Explosion, a pastor was bursting with excitement because he saw angelic beings hovering over the Met Center? He was not the only one who spotted God's angels. We received the following letter after the Explosion:

"I had the opportunity and privilege to minister on a healing team at the Minneapolis Healing Explosion on June 6th. We heard and saw many exciting things that night and at the Victory Breakfast the next morning.

"After we had been singing for several minutes, I had a vision of a huge angel leaning casually on a sword beside the left side of the stage. Do you remember the black curtains behind the stage? Well he was almost as tall as those curtains. I was so impressed with his size that I called the Met Center and asked them the height of the curtains. They said that the curtains were fifty feet in height. He was one BIG angel!

"A few minutes later as we were singing the words, 'Blow the Trumpet in Zion', I saw a similar angel on the right side of the stage, and his sword was starting to come up! Someone started praying and thanked the Lord for the 'inhabitation of angels' there that night.

"When he said that, I thought, 'Yes, they REALLY are here, and things are REALLY going to be happening tonight!'

"Just before Charles and Frances entered the arena, I glanced back to the stage again. I saw more warrior angels!

"On the middle of the three carpet runners that ran the whole length of the arena, there were angels lined up on its entire length and they were each facing alternate directions!

"With that vision, I knew that we did not have to worry about anything that night. It was all in God's hand, and He had it WELL in hand! Also, I recognized that it was a very important night – not just for what we as believers perceived, but as being extremely important for the fruition of God's ultimate purpose.

"Bless you for your ministry."

During the training sessions at the Radisson Hotel South, the healing team trainees asked God to station angels around the Met Center. Several people saw the flood of angelic beings flowing en masse from the Radisson to the Met Center where the Explosion was held.

Over the years of the Healing Explosions, in every case, without exception, there were reports of believers sighting angels hovering like a heavenly umbrella over the great arenas or soccer fields where the explosions were to take place. We have been to arenas over thirty days ahead of the explosions, and the angels have been there. We believe that God would send them fifty days ahead for some reason unknown to us. Then on the day of the Healing Explosion, at the very moment the healing teams entered for final instructions, all the angels would descend into the arena. We don't know what they did, but we believe God used them to work with the team members in some way.

After one of the explosions, a lady reported that she was having a problem getting someone healed and she called a supervisor (they were identified with a blue ribbon). The man came to help, gave instructions which she applied, and the person was healed. She turned to thank the supervisor, and "he had vanished!"

On another occasion, angels blowing trumpets lined the roof of a large Assembly of God church, calling people in from the north, east, south and west! What a sight to behold as we left the freeway and caught sight of the building where we were to minister! Each day, as we drove to the church, the angels were very apparent. The pastor shared with us that at their prayer meeting two weeks prior to the Healing Explosion, they had all faced different directions and began calling people in from specific towns in all directions within a three hundred mile radius. How glorious it is to know that God assigns angels to specific duties in and around the areas where His Word is going to be proclaimed with signs and wonders following!

Rejoicing in Heaven

Can you imagine the rejoicing in heaven when hundreds of ordinary believers, modern-day disciples, all working in one accord, bring healing and deliverance to thousands in one night? As exciting as each and every miracle is the knowledge that each person who testified would say, "someone" or "a little lady" or "a young man" or "a healing team member laid hands on me and I was healed." What joy it must be to Jesus and the angels of heaven. Finally after 2,000 years, the body of Christ is arising in power and great glory to do the same miracles as were done by those early seventy, only now there are thousands instead of a few!

Healing Explosions were not and are not the end result of God's work in a city. They are but an explosive beginning. Those teams are now going out to spread what they learned – healing the sick, setting the captives free, bringing salvation to the lost and ministering the baptism with the Holy Spirit and making disciples of others to do the same.

Ordinary believers – construction workers, secretaries, teachers, doctors and businessmen – are working in God's power, to share God's best, to bring thousands to Jesus through their powerful witness with signs and wonders following, just as the Great Commission proclaims. How else can we reach the lost, the unsaved, the sick? Praise God, He has replaced ignorance with knowledge of the truth. The family of God must step out and believe what the word of God says and accept their ministry. Although God may not call you to a fulltime traveling evangelistic ministry, your ministry is equally important. Wherever God has placed you – at work, at school, at home – is your ground to plow, to seed and to harvest.

Chapter 7

Glorious Jet Lag

Several years ago, when we made a few trips overseas, I would come home each time so exhausted and suffering from jet-lag so badly that I made a statement to several friends, "I'll never go overseas again unless God writes me a special delivery letter and hands it to me in person!" Be careful what you say, because God hears your every word!

I really thought God mercifully excused me from traveling overseas because of the tremendous physical strain placed upon my body. Then I got healed of diabetes, and God brought that special delivery letter to me in person! He didn't write it on paper with a pen or pencil, but He wrote it on my heart when He told us to lip-sync the healing video tapes into Spanish as our first foreign language and then go to the countries where we would send them.

Bogota

God promised us that He had prepared spiritual sticks of dynamite which would set off an explosion around the world. The first stick of spiritual healing dynamite was set in place on December 14, 1986 at the Coliseo de Salitre in

Bogota, Colombia.   God's plan to spread the Miracle Evangelism message to all of South America was very apparent as church leaders from Colombia, Peru, Bolivia, Ecuador and Brazil converged for the first Healing Explosion in a Spanish-speaking nation.

From the moment the plane landed, we felt electricity in the air. We could feel and sense in our spirits that God was going to do something special. Our plane was two hours late because of authorities questioning some of the passengers as to the reason for their visit to Bogota – was it legitimate or was it cocaine? This only heightened our excitement about what God was going to do in Bogota!

Over 100 enthusiastic Colombian *cristianos* were waiting to greet *los Americanos*. They met us with outstretched arms and loving songs of welcome. Even though they were singing in Spanish, we easily recognized "I Love You with the Love of the Lord" and "Alleluia" as well as other songs with familiar melodies. Their love and anticipation were expressed in their tears, warm embraces and brotherly kisses as we made our way through the crowd which enveloped us from the plane to the waiting cars. Never have we been any place where we felt such immediate and tremendous love as we did there!

As we drove to the hotel, we were excited to hear what had been going on before our arrival in Bogota. Over 4,000 believers had taken the video training on *How to Heal the Sick*, but because of space limitations, only 1,600 were going to be able to attend the "live" training meetings scheduled before the Explosion.

The pastor shared how one group in his church, before they completed their training with the video, went out on the streets one night and began asking if anyone needed healing. A crowd began to gather, and before they finished, over 200 people had been healed. The exciting bonus was, 50 souls were saved as a result of the love of God demonstrated in the street healings. Miracle evangelism works!

During the final training sessions, due to the large number of churches which were involved, only a limited number of healing team members were allowed from each congregation. Each of them faithfully attended every training session, skipping meals and using the short breaks between sessions to grab a quick bite to eat and a room-temperature bottle of soda pop from food stands on the street. Because of the magnitude of the meetings, the Coffee Commissioner of Colombia sent out trucks to dispense free coffee. Wherever you looked during the breaks, you could see people praying for each other, some with one hand holding their free coffee and the other hand laid upon someone who needed healing.

Every training session was completely packed out, wall to wall! Their excitement to learn more and to be trained in healing was a delight to those of us who attempted to communicate in our inadequate Spanish and through interpreters.

The worship and praise was typical of the love of God which so deeply permeates the hearts of the Colombian Christians. They put themselves wholeheartedly into magnifying God, with hands and voices lifted to heaven, never seeming to tire and with wave after wave of adoration diminishing only reluctantly. We were all lifted up into the very throne room of God at each service.

To God Be the Glory

The Healing Explosion was scheduled for December 14, 1986 at 9 a.m. It had not been advertised until several days prior to the event. When we arrived at the coliseum, over 7,000 wild, turned-on Colombians were waiting for us! Many of them, not wanting to miss anything, stayed throughout the day until the last service ended at 9 o'clock that evening.

The music could be heard – and felt – a block away, and God used it to draw more and more into the Coliseo de Salitre to experience His power. The young people of Pastor Castellano's church both sang and danced in a beautiful panorama throughout both times of worship. Their voices, accompanied by enthusiastic clapping and cheering, were like a magnet which drew the crowd into their exuberance and created an energy that permeated the arena.

When we drove up to the Coliseo de Salitre for the first meeting, angels filled the coliseum so full that Charles sensed a "bulging of the walls" with the power of God. God always sends a mighty host of angels to every Healing Explosion, and this one seemed to outdo all others!

As we drove to the coliseum for the second Healing Explosion in one day, we saw people pushing wheelchairs for miles to get to the services. As we walked in, we were greeted with diseases that we had never encountered before, but there was also an excited anticipation in the entire audience that we had never felt before in any meeting.

Expectancy Draws the Supernatural

Every seat in the great coliseum was filled, and every aisle was packed solid with people. It looked like one giant sea of faces squeezed together like sardines, but full of faith and belief! The faith of one oozed over onto others! Many people were waiting outside, hoping to get in. It made our hearts cry out because of the needs that were there and the hopeless cripples we saw.

The praise service was already in progress as we arrived, and there was such a sense of everyone entering into complete and total worship of God and Jesus that you could feel the supernatural even while walking to the stage. The people were so excited about what God was going to do that they wanted just to touch us before we walked onto the platform. Believing that they would be healed, they reached out, and they were healed – the Healing Explosion was their point of contact!

As we reached the stage, the pastor asked us if we would mind laying hands on those in wheelchairs during the praise and worship. Our spirits leaped within us because we had been wanting to do this during our United States Healing Explosions, and here was our opportunity.

The worship paused just long enough for us to say a few words. We prayed over the microphone, then told them what we were going to do. We said, "When we touch each of you who are in wheelchairs or crippled, God's healing power will go into you, so get up and walk, in Jesus' name!"

As we stepped off the stage, we both prayed fervently, because the enormity of the moment became a reality in both of us at the same time. We told God, "God, if you're not in this, it will be a mess!"

We walked over to the first person in a wheelchair and, in very limited Spanish, I said, "Recibe su sanidad en el nombre de Jesus!" (Receive your healing in the name of Jesus!) Then I said, "Levantase!" which means "Get up!"

Neither of us could remember how to say the word "walk". I had studied Spanish fifty-five years previously in high school, but had never used the language. The Holy Spirit brought some phrases back to my remembrance, but the word "walk" just would not come into my mind. I whispered to Charles who also had studied Spanish for two years in school, "How do you say 'walk'?"

The Holy Spirit reminded us in a most unusual way. I doubt if there is anyone reading this book who has not heard the little song which goes like this: "La cucaracha, La cucaracha, Ya no puede caminar. Porque no tiene, porque le falta, marijuana que fumar!" Interpreted, that means, "The cockroach, the cockroach. Now he is unable to *walk*. (There was the word we needed!) Because he does not have, because he lacks, marijuana to smoke!" What a silly thing to come back into your mind at a time like this, but it worked!

Charles leaned over and looked at the man and said, "Camina en el nombre de Jesus!" This horribly crippled man immediately walked right out of his wheelchair as if he had never had anything wrong with him. The crowd went wild, and faith soared! My mind said, "He must not have been crippled like we thought!" Such faith! Obviously this was a work of God and not anything great or special in Charles or me, which ensures that God gets every ounce of glory!

We went to the second person and said exactly the same words, "Camina en el nombre de Jesus!" That person also walked right out of his wheelchair just as if nothing had been wrong with him. Faith ignited like matchsticks aligned in a row, and every person in the line became ablaze with faith!

We went to number three! Same results! Number 4, number 5, number 6 and right down the line until finally one person failed to rise from their wheelchair. We could hardly believe the gift of faith had so risen up in us. We thought, "What's wrong with you that you didn't get up?" But we went right on to the next person, and the flow kept going, as one after another got up and walked. At that point, our faith was so high that we both felt we could have done anything that Jesus had done, including walking on water!

A little girl with a broken back had been brought to the meeting on a stretcher. After we said the same words to her, she came off of that stretcher, and the next thing we knew, she was on the stage testifying to what God had done for her. Her little testimony brought tears to the eyes of everyone as she walked even in the cast that immobilized most of her body.

Then we got to a man both blind and crippled, who had been brought on a stretcher. As I stretched out my hand toward his eyes, my fingers were about three inches away when he screamed, "I can see! I can see!" In a matter of seconds, he was off his stretcher and on the stage glorifying God for His miracle power! It was a moment none of us will ever forget!

We didn't stop. We went right down the line, and as soon as they came out of the wheelchairs or dropped their crutches, we turned them over to the healing teams to help them exercise their new walking abilities! More than 100 came out of wheelchairs, stretchers and braces in one service!

Normally, when someone is healed dramatically or comes out of a wheelchair during a healing service, time is taken to tell the audience about the healing. However, the power of God was so strong on those who had come that we felt we could not waste even one moment but had to continue as fast as we could through the crowd while the power was so supernatural.

When we had laid hands on the last one, the reality of the greatness of what God had done fell upon both of us, and we cried like babies as we ran back to the stage. Everyone on the stage was weeping. As I reached for my purse to get a tissue, my daughter Joan said, "Don't bother, Mother, I've already used them all up!"

Manuel Ferrera, Assistant Superintendent of the General Council of the thirteen million Assemblies of God church members in Brazil, wept openly as he said, "Never in all my years of Pentecost have I ever seen anything like this!" And neither had we!

Shortly after this, some 4,000 people poured out of the crowd of about 11,000 to receive salvation and the baptism with the Holy Spirit. They ALL began to speak in tongues as the Spirit gave them utterance, and what a magnificent thundering of power reached into the heavens!

There was no way we could get the people back into the stands after the baptism, so we released the healing teams, who were by now even more charged with anticipation and faith than they had been at the training sessions! The teams moved as a mighty stream onto the floor and throughout the audience that remained in the stands. Healings took place like popcorn popping all over that crowded building!

Although time had seemed suspended for most of the Explosion, there finally arrived a lull, and the service began to draw to a gentle close. However, scores of people who were unwilling to leave without taking the power of God home with them, took pieces of clothing off and threw them at us for us to touch and return to them, believing that they would receive the promise of Acts 19:12, when pieces of clothing that had touched Paul's body were laid upon the sick, they were healed and the demons fled from them. Others reached for the hem of my garment and were healed because of their faith level! The same Holy Spirit power heals today as healed through Jesus and Paul.

The power of God exhibited in Bogota has made us shrink into oblivion as we stand in awe at the wonder of His majesty, glory and grace! You cannot stand in the presence of Almighty God and see His wondrous handiwork and be the same person you were when you came. And we don't want to be!

One Fire Lights Another

Just as a string of little firecrackers is lit and a chain reaction of popping begins, so the report of a mighty move of God creates a divine chain reaction. God promised us that Bogota would be like a stick of dynamite, not a tiny firecracker, and it would be the beginning of a burst of powerful life-changing explosions across South America.

Manuel Ferrera came from Brazil to Bogota for the Healing Explosion, and as he witnessed the mighty manifestations of God's presence, he wept.

He saw with his own eyes some eight to ten thousand people receive the baptism with the Holy spirit during the two Sunday services. He wept again as he saw over a hundred people jump out of wheelchairs or drop their crutches and walk out onto the coliseum floor praising God. Never had he seen the likes of this powerful manifestation of Jesus' healing touch.

His life forever impacted, he now wanted to do all he could do to carry the vision to Brazil and train all thirteen million Assembly of God church members. We challenged him to let us help him do the greatest miracle ever seen on earth!

When God put a world vision into our hearts eighteen months earlier, He conveyed to us that He wanted to set an example before the world of the swiftness with which He can reach all the world. The first stick of dynamite had exploded with great resounding effects that were going to ignite fires throughout the nations.

The next day, we went over the mountains to Cali, Colombia. Word had gotten to Cali before we did, telling of the wonderful miracles that happened in Bogota, and they were ready for a real explosion!

The crowd was so excited that they were almost impossible to control, even with the armed guards who patrolled the arena. There was a soccer game the same night, so many people thought there would be a small attendance, but the stands were crowded with people who believed God for healings. The news of signs and wonders spread quickly, and the press of the crowd was beyond anything we could ever imagine.

We could hardly wait to go down to the wheelchair section because our faith was at such a high level we knew God would perform miracles again. But word came to us that the police would not let us off of the stage because of the danger to us. The people were so hungry for God, the police felt they would stampede and we could be killed in the crush of the crowd.

Our hearts cried out. We wanted so badly to go down there and lay hands on the sick; then we heard the quiet voice of God over the enthusiastic praise and worship. He said, "What did I send you to Colombia to do?"

We responded, "Thank You, Father. You sent us down here to teach these people that if Charles and Frances can do it, they can do it, too!" God had given us one night of divine glory and allowed us to personally partake in the feast of miracles, and then He reminded us in His loving way that He wanted the ordinary believers who had been trained to know what they could actually accomplish in the name of Jesus and by the power of the Holy Spirit.

The Hands of God Multiplied

When the two of us laid hands on the people in the wheelchairs in Bogota, only one person came out at a time. But what happens when 500 people lay hands on the cripples at one time? We were soon to find out.

We explained to the crowd that the healing teams had been trained and could do exactly the same things that we could, because God is the Healer and He uses believers to be extensions of His hands. We instructed those on the healing teams to go to the wheelchair section. Then we told the people that when I said the words, "Silver and gold I do not have, but what I do have, I give you; In the name of Jesus Christ of Nazareth, rise up and walk" (Acts 3:6), the healings teams would lay hands on them and they should get up and walk! We reminded them that the healing teams had the same Holy Spirit power we have, and that there is no difference in the voltage!

The healing teams were in place. The people in wheelchairs were waiting with supernatural expectancy. Then I spoke the words that were electrifying as they resounded through the microphone to all the loud speakers of the arena: "SILVER AND GOLD I DO NOT HAVE, BUT WHAT I DO HAVE, I GIVE YOU; IN THE NAME OF JESUS CHRIST OF NAZARETH, RISE UP AND WALK!"

As the healing teams laid hands on them, people came out of wheelchairs just like they did in Bogota. They began running out to the center of the arena, and for a while it looked like complete pandemonium. Glory to God when pandemonium is caused by the power of God!

The first person who came out of a wheelchair was a paraplegic. His legs had been totally lifeless, and when the power of God hit him, he ran to the center of the arena and began twirling around in the center of the arena floor. His picture appeared on the front page of the newspaper the next morning! It was proof that "If Charles and Frances can do it, you can do it, too!"

When the call for the baptism with the Holy Spirit was made, over 6,000 came, and it was a night of Holy Ghost Pentecost. Most of them who received the Holy Spirit had just gotten saved, because 95% of them had raised their hands to show they had prayed the sinner's prayer for the first time that night. Signs and wonders will always be followed by a great harvest of souls!

The word which was so vividly placed into our hearts in early November, 1986, came to our remembrance: "Thus far in 1986 I have set the foundation. During the last two months of 1986 I will put the dynamite in place. During the first four months of 1987, I will set off an explosion which will go around the world, and THEN..."

We knew clearly what the "and THEN.." meant. Jesus said that all of the population of the earth would hear the gospel from ordinary believers with signs and wonders following. We heard Jesus say that every one of these believers and the ones they win to Jesus will be endued with the power of the Holy Spirit, will speak in tongues and will be a witness by doing the supernatural with signs and wonders following.

The Vision is Alive and Well

If we went to Bogota, and saw the miraculous, and then nothing happened after we left, we would have gone in vain. When Jesus ascended into heaven, it was not God's plan that a few evangelists would go to every person on the planet and heal the sick and lead them to Christ. It was a burning fire in our hearts that the plan of God was for one fire to light another until all the world was ablaze with the glory of God. As wonderful as it was to see bodies healed by the power of God in Colombia, what thrilled us beyond words is that they caught the vision, and it spread and spread and spread like a wildfire.

Jaime Roman, one of our interpreters for the Colombia meetings, testified of continuing miracles through an explosion his church held long after we had left:

"A nine-year-old boy born blind received his sight for the very first time. A deaf-mute was healed. A young boy who was abnormally short for his age wanted to grow to normal height. After a believer laid hands on him, God added three inches to his height! Many who came in wheelchairs were healed and walking by the end of the meeting!"

We have heard the trumpet! We have heard the announcement of Jesus that He is coming soon and we Christians must prepare for His coming! We are seeing what once seemed impossible as, through ordinary believers, sickness is turned to health, death into life, unbelievers into miracle workers, and pew warmers into active, power-packed disciples winning the world to Jesus!

Chapter 8

Ready Hearts in the Philippines

Every Healing Explosion has a different flavor. Each is distinct, and each has something unique to that particular explosion. In Colombia, it was astounding to watch the tremendous number of wheelchairs which were emptied. In Manila, we saw something totally different.

We saw a hunger in the hearts of people to actually get out and do the works of Jesus, probably more than in any other city or country where we have been. The Filipinos are not noted for their aggressiveness, and yet, in the area of healing and wanting to follow after Jesus, they were absolutely incredible.

Manila was exciting from the word GO! Just before we left the San Francisco airport to fly into the Philippines, we called our office to see if anything critical had come in that we should know, since we knew we would not be in touch with them for a week. The news we received was that there had been a coup in the Philippines and that the Christian television station had been taken over by the enemy!

We realized that stories can be blown out of proportion, but it was a moment of decision – do we go to the Philippines in the face of machine guns? Or do we stay on the safe soil of home?

We talked with the other members of the team who were going with us. No one wanted to retreat. We were all in the mode to advance. When we arrived in Manila, there was absolutely no problem that we encountered nor any hindrance to the work God had called us to do there.

The moment we arrived in Manila, the teams were ready to go! We did not have any meetings scheduled for that first night, so everyone went to do a little shopping at a nearby store.

However, when the teams got inside the store, they were so wound up they began talking about Jesus instead of deciding what they were going to purchase. Before long, they were laying hands on the sick instead of shopping. People in the large warehouse-style store were lying all over the place under the power of God. They were getting saved, baptized with the Holy Spirit, and healed as the members of the teams who had come with us laid hands on everyone who was sick, expecting signs and wonders to follow!

So many people were healed that the store owner asked the teams to come back the next day and then again for a third day and promised that they would bring in a lot more sick people for them to minister to!

I was in one store which had received a brochure with our picture on it. Shortly after I arrived, one of the sales girls brought out the flier, pointed at the picture and said, "YOU?"

I said, "Yes!" They wanted to know if I would pray for a lady, and I responded that I would be happy to do that. The lady was bent over with painful arthritis, and she was instantly healed by the power of God. All her pain left, and her back straightened completely.

Before I knew it, there was someone poking a finger through the curtain of my dressing room, and a sweet little voice was asking, "Could you pray for me?"

I peeked out and there was a lady with a huge goiter on her throat. She asked if Jesus could heal the goiter, and I answered, "Of course, Jesus can and He will!"

I laid hands on her, and for a moment, it seemed like she almost choked. Then she swallowed. She swallowed a second time, and there was absolutely no sign of the goiter left whatsoever.

Exclamations of praise and wonder moved quickly through the store, and before I could catch my breath, a lady came to me with two lumps on her breast. The faith level of the clerks was really high because they had heard a lot about the Healing Explosion and they were ready to believe for anything. The two lumps disappeared from this lady the instant I put hands on them.

There was another clerk who was pregnant, and I laid hands on her for a perfect baby and a fast delivery. Before long, they were coming up with headaches, big problems and little problems. There were approximately thirty-five people in the store, and we just had a little mini Healing Explosion right there on the spot!

The faith of the Philippine people is incredible. They just believe that if you touch them, they will be healed by the power of God. They are spiritually uneducated people for the most part. Most of them have no religious training. They don't really understand the Bible or who they are in Christ and the authority we have, but their simple faith is absolutely beautiful to behold. When people believe that way, miracles can really happen.

The day of the Healing Explosion was a beautiful, balmy south Pacific day. Anticipation was as high as we had ever experienced. When we had arrived in Manila and checked into our hotel, as we stood in our hotel room on the seventeenth floor, we had seen the angels high above the Rizel Memorial Coliseum, where the explosion was to be held. Now on the day of the Explosion, the angels had come down to the level where the people coming to the arena would be seated. Charles and I held hands and said, "Thank You, Jesus."

As we looked out of our window, we saw the healing teams as they began to gather for the great event. We saw the stadium begin to fill with the 600-voice choir. We saw the people looking ever so tiny, but knew that, in God's eyes, they were giants as they marched into position, ready to do the things He had commissioned them to do.

Finally, it was time for the service to start, and as we arrived, the praise and worship was tremendous. The Filipinos enthusiastically ministered the same songs we sing in the United States. A salvation message was given and the opportunity to pray the sinner's prayer. Then the call was given for the power of God in people's lives – the baptism with the Holy Spirit.

When we told them to come out of the stands onto the field for the baptism of the Holy Spirit, it was almost like a cattle stampede. We have never seen people run as fast as they did to receive the power of God. You could actually see the dust in the field rising as their feet pounded the earth. There was no slow poking; they were determined that they were going to latch onto God and the Holy Spirit and that their nation was going to become a mighty nation in the Spirit and power of the living God.

It can be very difficult to judge the size of a crowd in a large area. However, the American healing teams estimated that approximately 10,000 came and received the Holy Spirit into their lives. When they started speaking in tongues, there was a sound as of a rushing, mighty wind.

Our teams from America were the healing team supervisors for the Explosion, and they did an outstanding job, but the Filipinos really thrilled us with their spiritual aggressiveness. We watched healing after healing and person after person get out of wheelchairs. What a thrilling sight it was to see the healing teams, consisting of people from all walks of life, doing the work that God assigned all believers to do!

After several hours of the glory of God and what we thought was the close of the service, we went back to our hotel. From the seventeenth floor, we again looked down from our room to the coliseum below. Somebody forgot to tell the Filipinos that the service was over! And that is exactly the way it should be! There were still people laying hands on the sick all over the field, and the power of God was still working. Just as we were so thrilled to see the Filipinos working, think of the thrill to Jesus as He looks down upon His end-time church to see them obeying what He commissioned them to do!

Many hours later, the healing teams finally left, the lights went out, and the angels vanished. But the exciting reports and testimonies flowed to us for months and months. The Filipino teams held over fifty Healing Explosions on their own over the next year with signs and wonders following.

People once totally deaf received hearing. Cataracts dissolved. An eyeball was created where there was none. Cerebral palsy was healed. Indians in mountainous areas were delivered from demon possession. A child blind from birth received sight. Teams went into prisons, and hardened criminals were saved and received miracles. The lost, the poor, the rich, the sick, the maimed, Catholics, Protestants, Pentecostals – all were ministered to and spiritual fires were lit that caught up into ever-growing flames of the power of God.

Chapter 9

Into the Morning Sun

We left South America with nations ablaze with the power of God. In the Philippines, our hearts and souls were thrilled with the supernatural energy of healing teams continuing the works of God. Then, the Holy Spirit launched us eastward into Europe.

We had been told that the Finnish people were very cold and undemonstrative, and that we should not expect them to get excited, or to show much enthusiasm over spiritual things. What a surprise we received when we walked into our first meeting which was packed out with people, standing wall to wall.

The love of the people exuded from them to us. It was so strong they and we alike burst into tears by the power of the Holy Spirit. They rose to a standing ovation, and we were completely overwhelmed as we saw some of the most excited and exciting people we had ever met. A recent letter told us that they were still enthusiastically clapping at every offering time because I taught them about giving to God!

Anointed Clothes, Cloths and Candy

The book, *How to Heal the Sick,* had been published in the Finnish language, and they really responded to the teaching on the power of prayer cloths. The first day, there were probably seventy-five to one hundred items given to us for which to pray, but by the final day, we had huge tables heaped high with personal items brought to us for prayer. We laid hands on each one. A beautiful woman who attended every meeting cut mountains of prayer cloths so there would be plenty for every service, so we laid hands on thousands of little prayer cloths for healing, salvation and other needs.

At each service, we demonstrated the power in an anointed prayer cloth by laying one that we had just prayed for on a sick individual. An infected ear stopped draining and quit hurting instantly. A frozen arm was loosened when we laid the anointed prayer cloth on it.

At one service, we told the story of R.W. Schambach "wearing candy", and it so touched their hearts that they started bringing candy for us to pray for, and before we left Finland, we prayed for hundreds of pounds of candy! Licorice is the favorite candy in Finland, and we never saw such piles of licorice in our entire life. Miraculous candy reports came back to us long after we returned to the United States!

The Empty Is Filled

Europe has some of the most beautiful

churches in the entire world, designed with expensive marble and gorgeous stained glass windows, but empty of people! The state church in Finland is the Lutheran Church, and we rented one of the large ones for our final meetings there.

This huge church could hold up to 1,200 people. The attendance board indicated only twenty-eight people had attended church the previous Sunday and that was the normal attendance. Can you figure out why? There probably had been no power of God demonstrated in that ornate, beautiful building for decades or maybe even for centuries!

But something happened in that glorious building when the people heard that the glory of God was going to show up! Word had gone through the town about our miracle service. One hour before starting time, they had to close the church and bolt the door. 1,400 people had jammed themselves on the inside of a building with a 1,200 capacity. Their excitement was a pulsating force of energy as they fervently prayed for God to move in their midst.

God has a different agenda in different places. One of the first miracles was when a well-known drunk got saved and was immediately delivered from alcohol. He was totally "spaced out" when he came forward, but with his salvation came an instant sobering up! This was a sign and wonder that the Finnish people wanted and, perhaps, needed to see, as many people throughout Europe are bound by alcohol.

A crippled man with innumerable back problems hobbled forward and was instantly healed by the power of God. Then came a word of knowledge on deafness, and approximately forty people received perfect hearing. That was followed by a succession of miracles which, when the service was over, produced an overflow of praise and rejoicing throughout the entire city.

It takes miracles to get a country turned toward God. Jesus said, *"If I do not do the works of My Father, do not believe Me; but if I do, though you do not believe Me, believe the works..."* (John 10:37-38).

According to an article in a paper given to us on Fin-Air, Finland has the highest suicide rate in the entire world, per capita, especially among young males. After having the entire audience repeat the sinner's prayer, I had all the men under thirty-five stand and promise not to commit suicide! It created quite a stir, but I believe that lives were saved that night for the glory of God!

Who Knows What Happened?

Two years later, we went back to Finland for another round of tremendous healing services. As we entered the building, I spotted someone rushing toward me with hands waving and exclaiming something which I could not understand. As she got closer, I recognized that it was the woman who had cut up those innumerable prayer cloths for us on our first visit. She came running out onto the arena floor and almost broke my ribs because she hugged me so tightly. She was laughing and shouting, "Kiitos! Kiitos! Kiitos!" along with other Finnish exclamations. Finally I got an interpreter, and then I realized why she was so excited.

She said, "Thank you, thank you, thank you for coming to Finland when I was so sick and was not expected to live. I will never forget your love as you came to my bedside and stayed with me four days and nights holding my hand." She continued, "But it almost broke my heart, when the doctors told me that I wasn't going to die, that you walked over to the door, waved at me, and said, 'Goodbye,' and then you just vanished."

I told her I had not been there and, in fact, had not been back to Finland at all since our first meeting two years prior. But she insisted that I was there with her for four days and nights, by her bedside, and there was no changing her mind. I didn't remember a vision, or a dream, or anything which could explain her seeing me and thanking me so passionately for being with her until she was told that she would live and not die.

There was simply no explanation, other than a miracle of God, a translation of my spirit or body, or God stopping time like the time He turned the sun back ten degrees on the sundial, or the time He stopped the sun, moon and stars for twenty-four hours. Perhaps today's astronomers have not discovered any such instance in this century or it would have been reported, but something definitely happened, and it was as real to that

precious woman as the words on this page. Glory
to God!

Chapter 10

A True Irish Miracle

We were invited to the lush, green island nation of Ireland by Annie Fitzgerald, creator of the fabulous "Dear God" items, and were privileged to stay in her home and minister to individuals the very first day we were there. One of the greatest highlights was that not one single person who came to the door unsaved left without knowing Jesus and receiving the baptism with the Holy Spirit. What a day of rejoicing!

Sometimes we wonder what a miracle really is. Is it just healing, or are other things equally miraculous? We feel there are miracles happening all the time if we will just give credit to God for everything that happens.

Ireland, being predominantly a Catholic nation, has their churches occupied at all times with people coming in, praying, and then leaving. Annie, her mother, and friends kept someone at the church all day long, inviting people to come to her house for healing and whatever other needs they had. We had one person after another arriving all day long, but what excitement to see their needs met!

In the evening, twenty little girls from a Catholic school came over to serenade us. They were all born again, but only one had received the baptism with the Holy Spirit. We ministered the baptism with the Holy Spirit, and they ALL received. Not only did they speak in tongues, they all left the house singing in tongues as they walked down the sidewalk to their homes.

One of the little girls was very bashful and cried when we began growing out arms and legs. But she was taking in everything that we had taught the children. The next morning, her mother came over to report that her daughter had come home and announced that she spoke in tongues and could now heal her mother's back problem. As the little girl instructed, her mother held out her arms. When her daughter prayed, the arms grew out and the mother's back was healed!

Three more little girls came to Annie's house the day after we left, and each one received the baptism. All of those little girls began their own Bible study, went out healing the sick, and some of them have had visions!

In Ireland, alcoholism is probably one of their greatest problems. Our evening service was to be held in a discotheque, which was certainly an unusual venue for us! A sign had been hung across the street where winos were known to camp out, which read, "Miracle Service, Come and Be Healed!" We credit that sign with bringing to us one of the most interesting and unusual congregations we have ever had.

A man on the front row was smoking a cigarette and singing, "Oh, How I Love Jesus!" That was a first for us! We managed to maintain our composure during that scene, and then we noticed an unusual thing occurring as we began to do miracles. Those on the back row were drinking "stout", and every time another miracle happened, they motioned to the bartender to bring another round of drinks!

I had been warned not to say anything about drinking since it is part of their culture, but when I see the effects of alcoholism, it is hard to keep my mouth shut. So many of the people there were obviously under the influence of liquor that I asked the Holy Spirit to show me how to approach the subject, and He did. This is what I said:

"I understand your culture and I understand the customs of your country concerning beer, stout, whiskey and wine. I know your customs are different from ours in America. I want you to know that I am well aware of the differences in our customs, but the word of God is the same, whether you read it in English or Gaelic, and it says, 'Wine is a mocker, strong drink is raging: and whosoever is deceived thereby is not wise.'"

That is a super strong statement to make when the drinks are free-flowing on the back benches of the meeting place! I could not say otherwise because I learned a long time ago to be a God-pleaser rather than a man-pleaser!

I could hardly believe the response. They literally ran to me asking me if they could be set free from the curse of alcohol. Old men, young men, women and even children knew they had a problem; and the Holy Spirit had convicted them by the words He gave me to say.

The last man in line was an obviously prosperous man because he was well dressed and did not look like a lot of the others there. I laid hands on him, and he fell under the power of God onto a sticky, beer-soaked floor. He had literally sucked the power right out of me when he fell. He stood up, brushed himself off, grabbed me and said, "Shure and begorra, I'll believe I'm delivered if you'll kiss me, lass!"

I remembered what Paul said, *I have become ALL things to ALL men, that I might by all means save some* (I Cor. 9:22). And you're right! I planted a kiss on his cheek, and he got saved! Glory! There's never a dull moment in the life of a miracle-working believer!

Chapter 11

Fake Shoes but Real Power

When you think of Holland, what comes to your mind? Most of us think of wooden shoes and fields of tulips. Charles and I remembered seeing paintings of little blonde-haired children wearing unbending, odd-shaped shoes of wood and were interested to learn that Dutch people do not really wear wooden shoes except for festive "clogging" dances and an occasional farmer. The wooden shoes are produced primarily for tourists to take home and display on their bookshelves or fill with artificial flowers. There is much more to the country of Holland than wooden shoes and tulips, and there was a special anointing upon the little Dutch children we met – who did not wear wooden shoes.

In the healing service, little Naomi fell under the power of God and lay there for about fifteen minutes. Sometimes people pop up immediately after going under the power, and sometimes they stay down longer when God is doing a special work in them. When Naomi got up, she said, "Mommie, I saw Jesus!"

She described Jesus as standing there with His arms outstretched, loving everybody. She said He had white hair and was beautiful. The next day, she was looking at some pictures in a Bible and said, "Mommie, Jesus doesn't look like that at all!" Hallelujah! I have always thought that most portraits of Jesus looked sad and broken and discouraging. I picture Jesus as strong and virile, passionate in His love for every human being, having a joyful countenance and a hearty laugh. Could that be the Jesus that Naomi saw? I hope so!

At that particular service, more than two hundred small children ranging from the ages of two to eleven received the baptism with the Holy Spirit. Many parents underestimate the ability of children to respond to spiritual things and to understand the moving of the Holy Spirit. But children are alive unto God and very receptive to the Spirit of God.

One little girl around twenty to twenty-four months was being held by her mother and was sucking a pacifier. When the time came for the children to respond to the instructions for receiving the baptism of the Holy Spirit, the mother grabbed the pacifier out of the child's mouth, and the little girl instantly began to speak in tongues!

We had another children's service, and more than three hundred children received the baptism with the Holy Spirit. God is moving among the children, so parents, BE READY! These are the days when YOUR sons and daughters will prophesy. Let us all make sure that our children are capable of prophesying in these end times. Every parent has a responsibility to their children to see that they are trained in the things of God at an early age and that they receive the power of God through the baptism of the Holy Spirit.

Revival came to the grownups, as well. More than 2,000 people were saved and baptized with the Holy Spirit. Hundreds were healed, and four children saw Jesus.

One of the most outstanding happenings was during the final night when we had a deliverance service. Homosexuals, drug addicts, alcoholics, lesbians and people totally bound with fear came to be delivered; and they got what they came for. More than five hundred came to the large stage on that momentous night. As we took authority over the devil, it looked as though the bones had been removed from their bodies. They all crumpled to the floor, slain by the power of the Holy Ghost and looking as if they had been hit with a bolt of lightning from heaven.

God Honors Ex-Convicts

A pastor traveled from Belgium to bring two ex-prisoners to the Holland meetings. He later sent us the following information which made our hearts leap with joy, because God is no respecter of persons. He always honors a gift from the heart.

"I am a minister of prison in Belgium and was several times with a few ex-prisoners in your meetings. Two of our boys have experienced a miracle in their lives. One was an alcoholic and was totally at his end. He was just a few days in our home and went with us to the meeting. Just before the invitation, he disappeared suddenly, but we found him back hidden behind some cars outside. Finally, he went back with me inside and you prayed for him. Now he has totally changed. He isn't scared anymore. (Before that he was so scared.) And even his face is totally changed. Praise God.

"A second man came free from prison but he still had to pay one-third of all his fines. And that was really a lot of money. He is jobless, and the government pays him a little but it is too little to pay all his fines. If he couldn't pay, he had to go back to prison. So there was almost nothing left to spend.

"One night, Frances said something about offering and that really touched him. So he gave all he had and there was nothing left for the entire month.

"The other day, someone came to him and gave him BF5000. That was one hundred times as much as he gave. Jesus did this, Hallelujah! He paid some of his fines. But God also encouraged him to trust Him for the rest of the fines. And God went on blessing him. Normally it is almost impossible for an ex-prisoner to find a job. The next day he was offered a good job! This is incredible!"

Just Like Charles and Frances

God has given us a message to take to the world, to get the believers out of their comfort zone and doing what Jesus did. Holland responded beautifully.

A single little flier brought some remarkable miracles in Holland. A woman had one of those little posters on the back of her bicycle to advertise the meetings. She had been through the trainings and had learned that, "If Charles and Frances can do it, you can do it too!" God promptly arranged a divine opportunity for her to put what she had learned into practice.

As she steered her bicycle out of the flow of traffic and over to the sidewalk, a young man from Denmark approached her and asked in English, "What does that sign say?"

She replied, "It tells about miracle services that are going to be held at the Kom en Zie Church."

He said, "The world is terrible. There are so many problems that nobody knows what to do. A group of us came down from Denmark to see if we could discover the real meaning of life. Some of us went to Amsterdam, some went to Utrecht, and some of us have come to Rotterdam trying to find the answer to life."

The woman's heart raced as she jumped at the opportunity to witness to someone. She replied, "I have the answer! His name is Jesus. He can give you peace, joy, and happiness. My husband just left me for another woman, and I have four children and no money, but I have peace, joy and happiness."

He pursed his brow thoughtfully and asked, "Where can I meet this man, Jesus?"

Her palms were sweating now. She thought, "I'll invite him to the meeting tonight. When he listens to Charles and Frances, he'll get saved and find the answer!"

Then the Holy Spirit reminded her of what we said, "If Charles and Frances can do it, you can do it, too!"

She straightened up, took a breath and confidently responded to the man, "Repeat after me..." and she led him in a sinner's prayer. Then she said, "Now slam the door of your heart shut, lock it and throw the key away so Jesus can never get out of there." (She remembered what we had told the crowd!)

God wasn't finished, and He reminded her of the next step. She explained how Jesus had died for our sins, had gone to heaven and had sent back the Holy Spirit to give us power to live the Christian life.

A brand new Christian, born by the Spirit of God is the most receptive they will ever be. So this young man immediately asked, "How do I get the Holy Spirit?"

Again, she was tempted to ask him to the meeting, where Charles and Frances would give a call for people to be baptized with the Holy Spirit, and he would go up and receive. But again the Holy Spirit prompted her about believers doing what Charles and Frances did. She asked, "Have you ever heard anyone speak in tongues?"

"No," he replied.

So she spoke in tongues for a moment. As she

paused, he exclaimed, *"What* did you say?"

She answered, "I don't know. I was just praising and worshiping God in an unknown language."

He began to argue with her, and finally he said, "You were not worshiping God, because you were speaking directly to me. You said, 'You are to take the message you have just heard to all of Denmark, and through your efforts, it will spread into Russia and then down into Western Germany'." He continued, "You were not speaking in tongues, you were speaking in Danish!"

The woman didn't know a single word of Danish. God had supernaturally given her a message for this young man in his own native language which he understood clearly. She then laid hands on him to receive the baptism, and he immediately spoke in tongues! God called a chosen servant and then equipped him all in a moment of time, using an ordinary believer to deliver a supernatural message!

Chapter 12

Miracles Are Easy

When God changes lives supernaturally, the word speeds more rapidly around the world than you can keep up with it! We received more invitations to minister throughout Africa than we could count, but it was impossible to respond to every invitation. We finally packed for South Africa and were thrilled so see the faith of the wonderful African people. They came to our meetings expecting God to do the supernatural, and when you expect God to do the supernatural, miracles are easy!

A girl who had been involved in a motorcycle accident just a week before attended one of our first meetings. Her neck was in a stiff metal collar. Her skull and vertebrae at the back of her neck had been fractured. She had been told she would have to remain in the neck collar for months.

When she first had the accident, it seemed as though there was nothing wrong; but before the day was over, her one entire side became paralyzed, and her arm and leg drew up. This was when they discovered the fracture.

Charles laid hands on her, and she fell out under the power of God and was there on the floor for a considerable length of time. When she got up, she ripped the collar off her neck. She twisted her neck in every direction, and every bit of pain and every bit of any associated problem was totally healed by the power of God. She could hardly contain herself and announced to the crowded auditorium, "I'm going to the doctor tonight, and I am going to tell him about my healing!"

She went to her doctor at 11:30 that night and got him out of bed to verify the healing! He was not really happy about being awakened, but he had to admit that the power of God had done a miracle work in her neck.

We discovered there were many people who had stuttering problems in South Africa, and we witnessed person after person healed completely of stuttering. What a joy to see their tongue released totally for the Lord!

In Empangeni, there was a lady who had polio when she was a baby and had been crippled on one side of her body all of her life. When she was ministered to, her leg grew out and her arm grew out. She came back the next night to tell us that, for the first time in her life, she had awakened that morning without pain in her body.

We took a drive over to the tiny nation of Zulu, which is positioned in the interior of South Africa like a tiny hole in a large donut. That night, we had a word of knowledge on ear problems, and eight people came forward who had been born deaf in one ear. God opened every single deaf ear! What a time of rejoicing this was for the Zulu people!

Throughout South Africa, in Empangeni, in Johannesburg, Cape Town, Port Elizabeth, Zulu, Durban, the hungering for the baptism with the Holy Spirit was almost unbelievable. Service after service after service, it looked like half to three-quarters of the audience would come forward to receive the baptism. So many people came forward the first night in Empangeni for baptism in the Holy Spirit that we had no one left to lay hands on for healing. Four thousand people received the baptism with the Holy Spirit that night.

In Port Elizabeth, there was no place for the people to come forward in the town hall except to go up on the stage. There were so many crowded on the stage to receive the baptism with the Holy Spirit that we had to pray the stage would not collapse under their weight!

Port Elizabeth was interesting because we really had very little to do in the healing line. The people realized THEY could do the same thing as Charles and Frances, and they began ministering to each other and getting people healed.

One young boy about nine years old met me as I came off the stage. He had a lower back problem and could hardly walk. He asked me if I would please heal him. He sat down, his leg grew out, and his back was instantly healed.

The most exciting part of the story is that he got the message, "If Charles and Frances can do it, I can do it, too! As I was laying hands on other people down the line, I turned around and saw him laying hands on a big Zulu man who stood about six foot two. That man was totally healed and fell under the power of God. What a joy that this little nine-year-old boy caught the vision and continued to minister to people down the line!

Sometimes people find unique ways to receive what they need from God. In Durban, the chef at the hotel accepted Jesus as his Savior and Lord after hiding behind a screen to listen to me share my testimony. Then he went on to receive the baptism and fell under the power of God. After he received the power of God, he no longer felt he had to hide behind a screen!

Many, many people received heart healings. They returned to our services after we had laid hands on them for new hearts, to report that the pain they had suffered for years was totally gone.

Signs and wonders followed us wherever we went in Africa. When people are expecting, miracles are easy!

Chapter 13

On the Road with Charles and Frances

A Divine Appointment in Pittsburgh

What would you do if your fourteen-year-old son were dying? His parents took him to every doctor they could. They prayed. They laid hands on him. They called a Christian television station to marshal the efforts of the entire city to storm the gates of heaven in behalf of their son. But, in spite of everything, their son Jason was slowly disintegrating from a healthy, active teenager to such a weakened state that he needed wheelchair assistance to move about. He did not have strength enough to be on his feet for more than five minutes at a time and could barely hold his head up even when seated.

I did not know the above information when I first saw Jason. Charles and I were at a meeting in Pittsburgh, Pennsylvania, and as we were sharing at the beginning of the service, I could not help but notice the young man sitting at a front-row table. All I could see of him was a mop of red hair resting on the table. During the praise and worship, he never lifted his head, he never stood up, he never did anything! I wondered – was he a super rebellious teenager who had been dragged to the meeting? Was he sick? Was he just mad at someone?

Because I saw no response from him to anything that was done nor to anything Charles or I said, I spoke to someone at the same table and asked, "Would you mind tapping that young man on the shoulder?" The person did, and Jason lifted his head up for the first time. I saw he was just around fourteen or fifteen years of age, and I asked him, "Honey, are you sick?"

His reply stunned me. He said, "I'm dying."

I quickly replied, "Then you better get up here real fast!"

He got out of his chair and walked the few steps necessary to get to the platform. As he approached, someone shouted from his table, "He's got a cancerous tumor floating through his body!"

I laid hands on him and cursed that foul spirit of cancer, and cursed every cancer cell in his body and commanded the root and seed to die in the name of Jesus. He dropped to the floor under the power of God.

His mother ran up to the stage, and I said, "You might as well join him," and she fell under the power of God, too. Then the unusual story began to come forth from various people in the room.

Jason was the son of a local pastor. After he contracted this disease, he had rapidly gone downhill physically. He finished his school year in a wheelchair because he had no strength to walk from classroom to classroom.

Medically, everything had been done that was possible, and he grew progressively worse. Finally, in desperation, doctors ordered an experimental medication from the research laboratory of a university, which cost $6,840.17. CAT scans were done on him for five days in succession, at a cost of $4,000.00 per day. Jason's family was not wealthy. They did not have money for these expenses, but they were willing to do anything and sacrifice everything to get their son healed.

Everything failed. He continued to deteriorate.

One Sunday night, Jason's father had a vision. In the vision, he saw me call his son out of an audience to lay hands on him. He saw his son fall under the power of God and get up totally healed! The vision was so real to him that the next day, he called the president of a local Christian television station to find out if they knew when we would be coming to Pittsburgh. The TV station president advised him that we were in town that very night, and gave him directions how to get to the meeting. They couldn't get a baby-sitter for their other children, so the father stayed home while the mother brought Jason to our meeting.

Jason lay flat on the floor under the power of God for what seemed an eternity. The audience sang a few worship songs, and he was still on the floor. We sang a few more songs, and he was still on the floor. Then I finally decided to take the offering. I spent a considerable amount of time because I always teach before I receive the offering. Jason was still on the floor, under the power of God.

Suddenly, what looked like a dead person sprang to life! Jason jumped to his feet and took off running across the front of the platform. All the while he was saying, "I feel cool! Man, I feel cool!"

We certainly didn't know what he meant until his mother explained, "His body temperature has been running three to four degrees above normal, and he always felt hot inside. She said this was the first time since he got sick that he felt normal, which to him meant he felt cool!

His pulse had returned to normal from the extremely fast rate he had experienced during the months of his sickness. It was then that Jason's mother shared his father's vision with me. There was no doubt in my mind that he was completely healed!

I called their house the next day to find out how Jason was doing, and although I made call after call, the line was always busy. Finally I was able to get through around six o'clock, and learned that he had been outside all day long helping his father paint the house. This is the young man who, less than twenty-four hours earlier, was slumped across the table and unable to stand on his feet longer than five minutes without passing out!

Jason went back to school the next fall and made the football team! He has had absolutely no recurrence of any form of the disease. Truly, we serve a wonderful God!

His healing was the kind we wish we saw all the

time, because it was an instantaneous miracle! All the symptoms immediately left, and I had him go with me to lay hands on the sick at the end of the service. Then I instructed him to do the same thing at his father's church the next Sunday.

To have the privilege of being a part of and watching as a miracle happens is one of the most soul-stirring things you can ever experience. There is nothing greater than seeing God move, whether it is in salvation, deliverance, the baptism with the Holy Spirit or healing. But, as we instructed young Jason, what thrills us the most is to see the body of Christ out there doing the same things today that Jesus did and commissioned each of us to do!

Angels of Love in Minnesota

We ministered in a school auditorium in central Minnesota in the dog days of summer. The school had no air conditioning, and the temperature was between 100 and 104 degrees with no ventilation in the building. Needless to say, it was extremely uncomfortable.

Because of the tremendous heat, the crowd was not the usual size. All of the balcony seats were empty. At least they were empty of people. During the service, we glanced up into the balcony and saw every seat up there was filled with an angel.

When the audience came forward to receive the baptism with the Holy Spirit, it was as though God released the angels who were sitting in the balcony and dispatched one to every person in the audience. These were small angels who appeared to be somewhere between three and four feet tall. Each angel reminded me of the Australian koala bear because they sat on the shoulder of each individual. Each person had their own special angel hugging them and hugging them and hugging them while an explosive message from the Lord came forth.

God said, "You may not understand what I'm talking about when you receive the baptism with fire. You may not understand why it was necessary for you to be purified with fire. You may not understand the supernatural things I am doing, but I have stationed with each one of you a special angel to help you and to guide you as you walk through these new waters which I have called you to tonight. These angels will not leave you nor desert you because I have stationed them with you on a permanent basis," saith the Lord.

It was one of the most unusual sights I had ever seen. Each little angel was just loving the person to whom they were assigned in an unbelievable and incredible manner. Many people saw the angels come out of the balcony and come down to minister to the people there. Not always do people see what is going on in the spirit realm, but there was an unusual number who saw these angels of love.

From Mental Institution to Ministry

In Marquette, Michigan we saw some of the most supernatural miracles we had seen in all of our ministry. One stands out because of the tremendous difference a touch from God can make in a person's life.

A woman came to our meeting who had been in a mental institution for many years and had escaped three weeks previously. She was spotted by two young college students as she was standing out in the lake with the water right up to her eyeballs, ready to commit suicide.

The young men rescued her, ministered to her by the power of the Holy Spirit and led her to the Lord, then took her to church. She had been on crutches for twelve years and could not walk without them. When hands were laid on her, God healed her instantly of arthritis in the knees and several other problems. The moment she realized she was healed, she broke forth in praise to God, joyously threw her crutches up in the air and told the pastor to keep them for a souvenir!

Because we were preaching the message to the body of Christ that God is trying to get every believer out of the pews and doing exactly the same things Jesus did, we called upon this new baby Christian, who had only been saved for three weeks, to heal somebody with a severe back problem. She followed our instructions and ministered with authority. She had the person line up their toes and look straight forward as they stretched out their arms. Then she commanded the arms to grow out. The arms were about two inches different in length. As the arms grew out, this lady, a former mental institution patient, began screaming out, "I did it! I did it! I did it!" The joy and excitement on her face was enough to draw the attention of heaven, and I believe the angels were rejoicing with her.

How we wish the entire body of Christ could get the message that we all are to go out and do exactly the same things Jesus did. What an explosion will take place in our churches when we all understand and act upon that revelation!

Rushing Mighty Winds in Sioux Falls

We will never forget a certain convention in Sioux Falls, South Dakota. The first night of the convention, we were in a tornado alert, so we took authority over the weather and commanded the tornadoes to go up into the sky and dissipate.

The next morning on the local televised news, the announcer said Sioux Falls had received a miracle, because the tornado which was heading directly for the city suddenly lifted up into the sky and dissipated! Glory to God, He answers all kinds of prayers!

The next night, we did not hear a weather report, but when we got to the meeting, the worship had just begun when the hotel manager came running into the room and exclaimed, "Everybody to an inside wall! There's a tornado in the vicinity, and a tornado watch is on." We learned later that when you are instructed to go to an inside wall or hallway, the tornado is really close and expected to touch down.

People ran quickly to the inside walls, where we

were told to face the walls and place our hands on them. Charles immediately said this was going to be a "wailing wall" but not one where we cry out for the Messiah to come, because we knew He had already come, but a wall where we were calling out to Him for divine protection from the storm.

We stood there and prayed in tongues for a good thirty minutes before the "all clear" signal sounded, and many people received the baptism with the Holy Spirit as a result of this experience. It is amazing how fast people can want everything God has for them when they're in the middle of a crisis situation! There was no damage to the hotel, nor to the cars of any of those who were in the hotel, although the tornado dipped down and damaged property a short way down the street.

A praise service really gets turned on when you have been delivered from a tornado! Then, as the people thanked and worshiped God, miracles exploded. A man whose arm was in danger of being amputated was totally healed. A woman with scleroderma, the disease which turns a body as into stone, was instantly healed. Hundreds and hundreds came for the baptism with the Holy Spirit.

Second-Honeymooners in Iowa

We received a letter after ministering in Iowa which really demonstrates how much God is genuinely interested in every part of your life:

"Here is one of the many miracles which took place while you ministered in our town. A couple in their sixties have been coming to our fellowship for a few months. In that time, they were both saved and asked for the baptism with the Holy Spirit. He, however, did not receive tongues. But, through your ministry, he received that fulfillment. For two years they had not had sex. She had a bad heart, and he had difficulties himself. After the healing of her heart and his release with speaking in tongues, they are proud to say they have a new and exciting marriage!"

Kick Me!

This couple had come a long way to attend the Chicago healing service. They had never been to a charismatic service and stood there wondering what it was all about as the praise and worship virtually raised the roof of the church. The singing and the exuberant participation from the congregation brought a tremendous presence of God during that wonderful part of the service.

Then came the offering time, and they admitted they had never seen people so joyous about giving, but God had ordained all of this to prepare them for the most unexpected of all – their healings!

The husband had broken his back and was sitting in a wheelchair. I stepped down to him, laid my hands on his back and commanded a new spine to come into being. Then I said something as I stood in front of his chair to let him see that God had answered his prayer. I said, "Kick me!"

To everyone's amazement, including both his and mine, he immediately kicked out his leg! I said, "If you can kick that leg, then you can stand up, so in the name of Jesus, stand up!"

He stood up!

Then I said, "If you can stand up, then you can walk, so in the name of Jesus, walk!"

The place was so jammed with people it was almost impossible to go anywhere, but because he had discovered he was healed, he stood up, began to walk and actually made a path for himself. The audience roared with excitement, and his wife turned up her oxygen because she was so excited she was using up her remaining supply. She had emphysema and had already used up one and one-half tanks of oxygen. She knew she had to have that last half tank in order to get her home. But God had other plans.

It was easy to discern they were not saved, so we led them to Jesus immediately, because it is hard to turn down Jesus after you have had a miracle. Then we laid hands on her for total healing, and she fell under the power of God, got holy laughter and was completely healed of emphysema. She was laughing so uncontrollably that, if she had not been healed, she would have needed an ambulance! Needless to say, she did not need her oxygen tank on the way home or, to our knowledge, ever again.

To someone who has been a Pentecostal for years, the above might not seem so supernatural, but when someone who has never experienced the supernatural ends up receiving two incredible miracles and then gets a real dose of holy laughter, it is a night never to be forgotten.

They left the service with the wife riding and the husband pushing the wheelchair!

Chapter 14

Riding on a Whirlwind

Charles and I have been based in Texas since our marriage, but we are close to what is called the "Tornado Alley" of the Midwest. Those gigantic whirlwinds come through like roaring trains, and people get out of their way and into storm shelters when possible, because the force of the swirling winds can suck up everything in their path.

The passion that God gave us for healing the sick and training ordinary believers to heal the sick created an uncontainable force of the power of God everywhere we went. And remember, we didn't even get started until we were over 100 years old! As we continued doing what God called us to do and the years of our age increased to 140, 150, 160... the energy of the Holy Spirit was unbelievable, and we have had many people over the years tell us that we out-run people one third of our age. Even now at 180 and no longer traveling "on the road", we still get up every single morning with praise and expectation to see what God is going to do *today*, and there is never a dull moment!

As we flew coast to coast and around the world, we often found ourselves coming home only to unpack and repack our bags. Every single miracle of God is written in His holy record book, which we believe is the Bible being continually written today by heavenly journalists, but we do not have the space to record all of even the most exciting miracles.   Let's just take a whirlwind tour of several cities which received a mighty touch of the power of God, and then we will feast on several really heartwarming testimonies.

Chicago

Chicago, the windy city, experienced the mighty winds of the Holy Spirit. People came by bus from all over the city. Some rode the elevated train across the Chicago skyline. Others drove all night from hundreds of miles around.

More than 4,500 responded to the call to be baptized with the Holy Spirit, streaming to the arena floor. A man born deaf in both ears was healed. Rheumatoid arthritis, ringing in the ears, spina bifida were gloriously healed.   Crushed bones and broken bones were knitted back together by the power of God, while dislocated bones and discs simply obeyed the commands of ordinary believers.   The demon-possessed were set free and went on their way rejoicing with their new-found freedom in Jesus Christ, speaking in tongues as tears rolled down their cheeks.

Anaheim

For three days, the ballroom of the Disneyland hotel rocked with the praises and cheers of God's army as they witnessed first-hand as well as put into practice the principles of laying hands on the sick and seeing them recover. Californians have always been noted for their boldness and their gregarious personalities. This crowd was no different. There was no shyness or doubt, no questioning, no self-consciousness. When they were released to lay hands on someone, the person to be healed knew that the power of God was coming at them full force.

At the anointing breakfast, a person actually collapsed and appeared dead. People were gathered to hear the "charge" and to receive the commission to the healing teams, when the person who collapsed created quite a stir. What an event to witness as the teams instantly surrounded the person and brought God's healing power on the scene. By the time physicians reached the table, the individual was seated normally and had regained their composure.

In the Healing Explosion, as the healing teams ministered, God healed diabetes and blurred vision, macular degeneration, numbness in the legs and began tangibly closing a cleft palate. He removed varicose veins and repaired torn cartilage which was scheduled for surgery.

A gentleman, probably in his late sixties, came to the service in a wheelchair as the result of a stroke. He had been paralyzed on the left side, and had difficulty speaking, but he came expecting to be healed. When the healing teams went to the wheelchair section, they cast out the spirit of death and commanded a new brain into him in the name of Jesus. The man immediately got up and walked, unaided. In fact, whenever someone went to help him, he vigorously pushed them away. Like a little child, he kept indicating, "I do it, I do it", as he was learning to walk again.

A small youngster whose mother was a member of the healing teams had been operated on for cancer of the brain. The child came riding in a wheelchair to which he had been confined for the past five years. He did not know the person who laid hands on his body and commanded a new brain by the Spirit of God in Jesus' name. All the child knew was he had come expecting God to move on his behalf, so when the healing team member laid hands on him, he responded like a tiger raring to go and get with it. He got up out of that wheelchair and walked all over the place!

A real macho-looking motorcycle rider had extreme pain from herniated discs caused by a motorcycle accident. When a healing team member spoke to the condition in Jesus' name and he realized all the pain had left, this biker bent, twisted and stretched every way he could and took off running up and down the stairs. He forgot all about looking "macho!"

Bell's Palsy – That's Easy!

Picture yourself in this next situation, as a twenty-nine year old Tampa man awaits his turn with a healing team member and these thoughts race through his mind:

"What can be done for a diagnosed case of Bell's Palsy? My eye closes when I don't want it to. My face twitches. The bones of my face seem lopsided. Is there any help for me? When I smile, my eye shuts and won't stay open. When will something be done to help keep my eye open? Who can help my face that is so distorted?"

Suddenly, it was his turn and he was asked, "What's your problem?"

He quickly answered, "Bell's Palsy!"

Later he related, "As soon as the words dropped from my lips, I realized the young men did not understand the magnitude of the disease, because they immediately got excited and said, 'NO SWEAT FOR GOD!' They did something they called 'TNT" (the neck thing). My face began to tingle and move and it's all OK now!" As he gave his testimony, he had a beaming smile, and both his eyes stayed open!

Tampa miracles were amazing, as are all miracles. Deaf ears opened, a teenager was healed from severe car accident injuries, ulcerative colitis disappeared and underarm lumps dissolved. Then there was...

The Hug of a Lifetime

After the Tampa Healing Explosion, believers continued obeying the Great Commission. In one of the churches where a healing school was in progress, there was a seventy year old woman (the pastor's mother) who had been injured at birth when the midwife pulled her tiny infant arm too hard at delivery. The arm, for all practical purposes, was useless, and the woman had carried it to her front all of her life because it would not bend. As a child, she had to endure painful exercises and casts year after year. She was not even able to dress herself without assistance.

The healing team showed the next one-hour segment of the healing school and then demonstrated the growing out of arms and legs. It is always exciting when people get involved and see and feel their own arms and legs grow and other people's limbs grow, because they realize the power and authority they have in the name of Jesus.

The last person to come forward for healing was the pastor's mother. The healing team laid hands on her and commanded her muscles, nerves, ligaments and tendons, vertebrae and discs to be adjusted because she had back problems. She walked with a cane and had leg problems, so they ministered to that area, plus ministered to the neck and shoulder for pain to leave. Last, because of the arm being lame, they laid hands on her and asked the Lord to "give her an overhaul." At that point, the woman fell under the power (which she did not believe in – but she now does!).

She remained on the floor basking in the power of God for quite awhile. Her son knelt down beside her and laid hands on the lame arm, commanding it to be healed in Jesus' name. As everyone's eyes were glued in her direction, she began to move both arms. When she realized both arms were freely moving however she wanted them to, she burst forth in praise to God, lifting both arms straight up in the air.

Everyone went wild because, as the pastor's mother, she was known by all the congregation. This little grandma, who a few minutes earlier didn't believe in falling under God's power, was so drunk in the Spirit that, for awhile, she still could not get up. When she did finally get to her feet, she was overwhelmed with the presence of God. She kept moving her arms up and down in sheer delight.

As she returned to her seat, without her cane, she placed one arm around her son's neck and placed her newly healed arm around her husband's neck and said, "NOW I CAN HUG YOU!" In seventy years she had never been able to do that.

Chapter 15

Long Distance Miracle

If you have any doubt about long distance prayer working, you won't have any when you finish this next chapter.

During the Portland Healing Explosion, we learned of the abduction and brutal beating of a Seattle pastor's young daughter. She had been left unconscious in a drainage ditch with her head under water. Initial reports claimed the child was brain dead.

Immediately all fourteen hundred of the healing team trainees joined us in binding the devil and speaking healing over the child.

During the Healing Explosion, a progress report reached the stage stating that the child was still in critical condition but her little bruised and battered body was at least responding. We again prayed, en masse, for her total healing.

Does "long distance" prayer work? Oh, yes! Jesus' power is not limited by walls or distance. Read this article from a local newspaper regarding her miraculous recovery:

HOSPITAL DISCHARGES ELLENSBURG TODDLER

"Describing Theresa Johnson's recovery as 'miraculous' and 'unexpected', doctors at Seattle's Children's Orthopedic Hospital agreed to discharge the Ellensburg girl this afternoon.

"A discharge panel of eleven health professionals reviewed the toddler's case Thursday afternoon and 'decided she had recovered almost completely and is ready to go home,' according to Dean Forbes, a hospital spokesman.

"The child has been hospitalized since July 30, after she was abducted and beaten near her Ellensburg home.

"Theresa's speech is not yet fully recovered, and she will need to continue seeing a speech therapist in Ellensburg. That, however, is the only therapy the young girl will need.

"Forbes said there is some concern the child's vocal cords were damaged during intubation. On two occasions a tube was inserted into Theresa's throat to help her breathe. Forbes said Theresa is scheduled to return to the hospital next week to have her throat checked."

In addition to the newspaper coverage, the local television station monitored the little girl's progress. The anchorman reported that many people had been praying for her complete recovery. Even the news media gave credit to the Lord!

Praise God! Prayer works, and distance is not an issue for God!

Chapter 16

If Your Heart Is Strong, Come Along

Here we are, Lord. Send us.

What an experience to see yourself on immense, mammoth billboards! Thirty of these "giants" announced the Healing Explosion in the city of Belem, Brazil. More than 10,000 posters and fliers were nailed to telephone poles, walls and wherever they could be hung all over the city. We saw ourselves coming and going.

The day we arrived, a downpour of rain had completely saturated the field of the open air stadium where the meeting was to be held. We were very concerned about the mud. However, God simply blew His breath over the field, and it was totally dry before the meeting began.

A tremendous air of expectancy surrounded all of us the night of the first Healing Explosion ever held in Brazil (July, 1987). There was even a beautiful rainbow positioned over the moon just before we arrived at the stadium. Everyone who saw it exclaimed, "It is a sign from God!"

Because South Americans are notorious for not being on time, we were encouraged to arrive late, but we were so excited we could hardly wait, so we left early! When we arrived, we discovered the stadium which holds 35,000 was already filled to capacity. The doors had been locked, keeping thousands of people on the outside. We panicked! We agreed that we did not come to Belem to lock people out. We insisted that the doors be opened and the crowd allowed to stand on the field of the stadium.

What a sight! Thousands of human beings filled the great field, packed in as close as possible to each other. Even with twenty-five Green Beret Police and trained counselors making a human chain across the front of the platform, the enthusiasm of the pressing crowd was so great that nobody could keep them back. They were hungry for what God had for them.

There was an estimated crowd of over 60,000 at that first great Brazilian Healing Explosion, and many more were turned away because there was no room.

After worship and praise, I read from a Portuguese Bible. A message reached us later that the people thought it was wonderful that I read the Bible in their language, even though my accent was "terrible".

After a brief teaching on the miracle-working power of God and how God wanted to heal them, we ministered salvation to the entire audience and called for the baptism with the Holy Spirit. There was no way the people could come out of the stadium seats onto the field because the huge soccer field was packed, but an estimated eighty percent of the people raised their hands to receive the baptism with the Holy Spirit.

While we were ministering the baptism, thousands of people began to pray in tongues. With close to sixty thousand people loudly and powerfully praying in the Spirit at one time, God's glory came down. God took over the service as His power literally exploded with a thunderous crack! The magnitude of God's power in that stadium was something none of us had experienced to that degree before, and it was actually almost frightening because it was so strong!

The people were excited about their new tongues, and they continued to pray. You could actually feel the power of God building and building and building.

I turned to Charles and said, "Honey, we just lost the service!" I knew in my spirit that was exactly what happened, so I looked at Charles while those sixty thousand people were praying loudly and fervently in tongues and I said, "Let's join them!.

We continued praying in the Spirit, and we could feel the power of God still increasing and faith igniting. After possibly fifteen minutes of praying in tongues (they don't stop like we do in America), I held up my hand for them to stop, and they thought I was waving at them, so they waved right back at me and continued praying in tongues, only they increased the volume.

I looked up at God and said, "God, what are we going to do now?"

We didn't have to do one thing. God did it all!

Suddenly an empty wheelchair went up in the air and was passed forward to the stage, then came another empty wheelchair – then came another wheelchair – then came a stretcher with no one on it – then came crutches – then came another wheelchair.

In the distance, somebody screamed, "She was blind and now she can see!" Then someone brought two children to the stage who had been deaf and their ears were opened and totally healed.

A scream rose from the audience at the end of the field. Our interpreter said the people were yelling, "Look at the orange shirt!" We had no idea what that meant, but our eyes searched the field until we finally spotted the man with an orange shirt. He was running around the outside perimeter of the field, with about a hundred people following him. The number swelled to about five hundred people trying to catch him.

After running nearly a quarter of a mile around the track, he ran up to the stage, hugged both of us and exclaimed, "I'm not even a Christian, and God healed me!" Then he added, "Please, I want to be a Christian!" We took care of that real fast! Then through our interpreter, we heard his story.

He had been in an automobile wreck about four years before, which had severed his spine, causing paralysis from the waist down. As he sat on the field, he began to feel life in his legs again and realized he could walk. Not satisfied just to walk, he ran, and he ran, and he ran!

God had done a second miracle to restore the atrophied muscles and lungs, and to supply strength for him to run nearly a quarter mile.

He went running and leaping and praising God! God is continuing the book of Acts through His disciples in this end-time generation harvest of souls!

We never regained control of the service because God's power just kept moving supernaturally through the people. Crippled bodies were made straight, and little children were healed by the scores.

One little girl managed to make her way up to the edge of the stage. Through an interpreter, I said to the pastor of the Assembly of God church, "You lay hands on her." He laid hands on this little child who had been injured in an automobile accident, and she was totally and completely healed by the power of God. Her damaged little legs instantly straightened out!

As we stood in the awe of what God was doing throughout the stadium, the tears that were shed were incredible. All of us who had come from the United States could do nothing but stand there and weep at the presence and power of God. The Assembly of God pastor wept like a baby and finally left the stage and just stood there and cried and cried. He kept sending me messages saying, "I have never seen anything like this in all my life." And none of us had either!

The pressing crowd surged forward into the stage area in spite of the security we had, and an entire cordon of police was necessary to assist us in getting through the people to the exits.

The thing that thrilled us as much as what had already transpired, was the fact that after we left and the crowd began to thin down, the healing teams had the space and opportunity to minister to the people.

A little boy whose body was totally crippled from cerebral palsy was healed by the power of God as a healing team member laid hands on him.

A child's skull which had not closed, closed instantly when another healing team member ministered. It didn't just start to close, but the entire skull closed completely! The mother had been told that her child was going to be mentally retarded. However, she felt confident that the supernatural power of God had totally healed the child.

There were many other healings that took place through the trained Brazilian healing team members after we left the stadium. What gave us indescribable joy was to know that after we left Brazil, believers would continue doing the works of Jesus.

Goiania, Brazil

The next day when we arrived at the Goiania airport, four people were standing on the airfield with signs that said, "Charles and Frances Hunter, We Love You. Welcome!" As we walked into the airport, a choir of over one hundred people greeted us with the most glorious songs we had ever heard.

All of us wept because of the love of these people and their desire to find more of God.

The night of the Healing Explosion was absolutely beautiful. God supernaturally sent doves to fly over the stadium, circling as though to say, "The Holy Spirit is here in this place." The next thing we saw was the stadium field totally filled with the presence of angels. At the same time, we saw the glory cloud of God descend over the area. We knew that once again God was going to do some tremendous things.

For reasons we do not understand, stadium officials have a tendency to lock the doors once the seats are filled. After much discussion, they finally opened the gates and allowed an estimated fifteen thousand additional people to come onto the field. With the stadium seats and the field filled to capacity, the crowd was estimated to be over 60,000, all with a tremendous hunger for the power of God.

It was another glorious night to remember! When the call was given for the baptism with the Holy Spirit, there was an explosion of the power of God. The beautiful Brazilian people were just like an empty sponge waiting to soak up the power. Can you imagine the sound of tens of thousands of people praising God in tongues at the same time? When that happens, there is POWER.

As the miraculous power of God spread through the crowd, people began passing crutches, canes and wheelchairs up to the stage. Because ministering to individuals was totally impossible, we instructed them to lay hands on whatever part of their body needed a miracle as we prayed in unison. Thousands and thousands raised their hands when we asked how many of them had actually felt the power of God in the part of their body that was sick. They were so full of simple faith, it was easy for them to be healed.

And the Demons Did Flee

At one point in the service, we bound the devil in the name of Jesus and commanded the foul tormenting spirits to come out of the people.

With 60,000 excited, expectant people praying in tongues along with our binding the devil and casting out demons, what happened next was inevitable. At the name of Jesus, those demons have to come out, and you never saw such a display of demonic activity in your life!

One demon-possessed woman started running toward the stage knocking everybody down that came within ten feet of her. She would pick up big men and throw them. Security quickly removed the platform steps to prevent her from getting up on the eight-foot-high stage.

After experiencing such a manifestation of the power of God in Belem and now in Goiania, I confidently said, "In the name of Jesus, you foul tormenting devil, I command you to come out of her!"

That didn't stop that devil one single bit! I repeated it, only this time I was a little louder and a little more emphatic.

She kept right on coming, throwing people out of her way. I must have repeated, "In the name of Jesus, you foul tormenting devil, I command you to come out of her" at least fifteen times, but she kept right on coming. She was getting closer and closer to the stage, just as devil-tormented as she ever was. By this time, my heart was beating a little faster than normal, and I repeated the command a little louder and a little more emphatic. She kept right on coming!

I'm going to be real honest with you. At a time like that, you can think of a lot of things in the twinkling of an eye, and probably the first thought the devil would have liked for me to believe was, "Is the name of Jesus really more powerful than the devil?" The second thought was, "Get behind Charles and let him protect you!" But I knew once I gave up control of the situation, everything was lost; so I stood my ground, even when she got to about two feet from where I was standing eight feet above her on the stage.

I didn't have time to say the whole command, so instead, I looked her right in the eye and commanded that devil, "In the name of Jesus, SHUT UP!"

Someone screamed at the side of the soccer field. I glanced over in that direction for an instant and, when I looked back, there was no longer a demon-possessed woman there. I wondered what had happened to her and didn't discover the real answer until about a month later when I was going through some pictures of Brazil. There was a series of pictures showing an opening in the crowd where this woman was throwing people around. The final picture showed this same woman, completely calm and in her right mind, her face reflecting the sweetest look of love you could ever imagine. No wonder I had not recognized her! The demons had finally given up and fled, and she was covered in the peace of God. I looked again and again. It was the same dress, the same hair, the same everything, except an insane woman was made perfectly whole by the power of God and the mighty name of Jesus!

An entire book could be filled with the amazing miracles which came about in Brazil by the power of the Holy Spirit. We had tremendous meetings in Sao Paulo where we received a detailed word of knowledge concerning a man who had been shot some eight years before, and he was totally healed from all the effects of the bullet wound. In Campinas, an aged blind man received sight and broke into shouts of praise, "Glori a Dios! Glori a Dios! Glori a Dios! Glori a Jesus!" What a beautiful sound!

The miracles went on and on and on. Glori a Dios!

We loved the people of Brazil, and they loved us. Their faith was uncomplicated, and they were able to receive easily from God. We estimated that well over 100,000 received the baptism with the Holy Spirit in this short series of Healing Explosions. There is no way to measure the number who were saved and healed, but great multitudes were touched. A part of our hearts was left in Brazil. When we returned home on Sunday, we were ready to go back on Monday if God had even hinted that He wanted us to go!

Chapter 17

Special People in Far-Off Places

God has blessed us with the privilege of meeting thousands and thousands of beautiful people, across the United States and on every continent – except Antarctica – and who knows what may happen down there before Jesus comes? Some of the people we met, we had a feeling that God just might use to influence a lot of other people in a big way. Here are a few international stories that still cause us to feel very humbled.

A Physician Learns to Heal in a New Way

We arrived in San Salvador, Central America, greeted by machine guns and policemen. However, they must have found us to be non-threatening because we had no trouble getting wherever we needed to go to do what God called us to do.

On Sunday morning, we had a miracle service at a Catholic church, and that evening we visited an Assembly of God church where remarkable things happened. The first healing was a woman who was in excruciating pain from two ruptured discs, who was scheduled for surgery. She was completely healed and literally felt the discs grow back into perfect formation in her body.

The next person on the stage was a man who also had severe back problems. Additionally, he had an incurable disease which caused tremendous pressure and pain behind his eyes and which would eventually lead to blindness. He was wearing bottle-thick glasses when he came up on the stage.

We ministered to his back first, and he was instantly healed! Then he said hopefully, "See what you can do for my eyes." We laid hands on his eyes and commanded that foul spirit of infirmity to come out in the name of Jesus, the blood and fluid to flow normally within the eye structures, and spoke healing and wholeness to both eyes.

When he fell under the power of God, his glasses flew off. Moments later, he jumped to his feet, pointed toward us and stated, "You are not a doctor, but I am. You cannot diagnose me, but I can." We were not sure what he was going to say next, but then he turned to the audience and declared, "As a physician, I am telling you that I am completely healed!" Not only was his back pain-free but his eyes were perfectly normal! Because of his former condition, he was being forced to retire from medical practice, but now he was restored in body and soul, with a bright and productive future ahead of him.

The audience rose to their feet in a standing ovation! Unknown to us, he was a very famous neurosurgeon whose sole purpose for coming had been "to inspect the meeting and check us out". When he saw the first woman healed, it ignited faith to believe for his own healing.

He received the baptism with the Holy Spirit then and there, attended our Healing Explosion training sessions the next day and was on a healing team at the San Salvador Healing Explosion!

The first person to whom the neurosurgeon ministered was a young man in a wheelchair who had been unable to walk. As a result of what the doctor had learned about healing and applied in faith, the young man was totally healed by the power of God and came right out of that wheelchair walking.

Surrounded by Shotguns

In Antigua, Guatemala, after one of the training sessions, we were privileged to meet the mother of the President of Guatemala. To reach her, we had to pass through her tight security system – several no-nonsense, rigid-faced soldiers carrying sawed-off shotguns.

She graciously ushered us into her chambers where we asked, through her interpreter, "Do you need God to heal you in any way?"

She answered, "Yes! I have a separated shoulder which was the result of an accident." We ministered to her in the name of Jesus, and she was totally healed!

Knowing she was a Christian, Charles began to talk about the baptism with the Holy Spirit, because we did not know whether or not she spoke in tongues. She told us with enthusiasm, "I would love to receive the baptism with the Holy Spirit!" When I ministered to her, she immediately began speaking fluently in her heavenly language.

Before we left this most delightful lady, we laid hands on her and she fell under the power of God. As we stood there, the same thought struck all of us: "What would happen if the guards came in here with those sawed-off shotguns and saw her lying on the floor?"

Praise God, the guards did not come in! But what an exciting time, and what an honor to be able to minister to such a wonderful woman!

Not Really So Stoic!

We hand carried the first twenty sets of Japanese video healing tapes to Tokyo. Where only one percent of the population is Christian, the hunger for God in Japan is incredible. Over two hundred pastors and leaders had gathered together for our one-night stop in Japan. When we were introduced to the pastors, the video tapes were turned on, and the first words the pastors heard us speak to them were in their native language.

After a few moments of video, I was given the microphone and, through an interpreter, I asked them if they would really like to know what the world says about the Japanese. I then repeated the question to make sure they really wanted to know! Then I said, "The world says that the Japanese are the world's best marketing people, and once they get the message of Jesus, it will spread rapidly over the entire world and then Jesus will be back!"

The people whom the world thinks are so stoic laughed so hard they almost fell off their chairs!

After our single night in Japan, we flew to Hong Kong for one meeting. The people there had never seen arms and legs grow out, and it completely astounded them. Some of the Chinese men crawled on the floor to get between the crowd where they could better see the miracles God was doing! The expressions of amazement on their faces brought joy to our hearts. A tremendous hunger was created in their hearts to learn how to heal the sick, and video schools began to spread all over the area.

From Hong Kong we flew to Manila where we were overjoyed to learn that over fifty Healing Explosions had been held since we were there a year earlier. One of the most interesting words God had said to us then was, "The talk of the streets in the Philippines will be Jesus! The conversations will not be of sin and the things of the world but will be centered on Jesus."

Each member of the American healing teams who had accompanied us had ribbons printed with the words, *Hunter Healing Team*, so they would be easily identifiable during the meetings. We told the teams to wear their healing team ribbons wherever they went, and the results were astonishing. The teams immediately discovered that they could not move two feet without someone walking up to them and asking for healing. Before they would finish with the first person, a line would form with others hungry for the healing touch of Jesus.

The same thing happened to all the teams as they wore their ribbons into department stores and restaurants. They had lines forming wherever they went. Truly Jesus had become the talk of the streets!

We flew home from the Philippines for just a day and a half before we left for South America. People have asked us how we keep from having jet lag, and we told them, "We leave town before the jet lag has time to catch up with us!"

And God Met Us Everywhere

Brazil awaited us with soaring faith! A woman who hadn't walked in thirty-two years walked to the stage totally healed. The deaf were healed and the demon-possessed were set free. Billboards and posters were everywhere, and the people told us, "As we go by your picture every day, we lay hands on it and pray for you." We believe that a lot of the results we saw in South America were because of believers who were praying for us.

From Brazil we flew to Cordoba, Argentina, where the very first morning, we ministered to the hotel manager and he was baptized with the Holy Sprit. He said he was embarrassed for us to lay hands on him in the restaurant for healing of his back, but we assured him we did this all the time, anywhere and everywhere. He knew one of his legs was an inch short and could hardly believe as he saw it grow out before his eyes.

The Multiplication Principle

Although the miracles in Cordoba were glorious, the most exciting thing happened when the healing teams went to work after we left the building! Our purpose in going to the nations was not to bring attention to Charles and Frances but to teach them that they can do it, too. The miracles which the healing teams reported were overwhelming and brought joyous tears to our eyes.

Two reporters from *Avida Abundante*, a Christian magazine which circulates throughout Argentina and Uruguay, interviewed us in Buenos Aires. One of them mentioned she had a painful problem in her spine. When we ministered to her, she indicated that all pain left immediately. Then I said, "Now I want you to practice on your friend."

We instructed her to lay hands on the second reporter's legs which were about one inch different in length, and instantly the short leg shot out. What was so interesting was her comment, "I did not believe it when it happened to me, but when I did it to my friend, then I believed." Then we told the second reporter it was now her turn to lay hands on their photographer!

The photographer had been in an accident which had severed the tendons in his left leg, and gangrene had done damage as well. He suffered great pain when walking. When the area was touched, he described the pain as electric shocks going through him. As Charles gave instructions in English and they were interpreted to the second reporter, she made the commands, and a creative miracle took place. When the photographer realized he had absolutely no pain, he spent the next few minutes jumping up and down on the healed leg because he was completely overwhelmed that a miracle had happened to him!

This is multiplication! Every believer needs to teach somebody else how to heal the sick.

As we packed our bags to leave Argentina, a report reached us that an exciting miracle had happened in Uruguay during one of the video training schools.

An ambassador in Uruguay had suffered the first joint of his little finger being cut off when he was a small child. After watching the teaching on creative miracles at the video school, the teams ministered to him and commanded the finger to grow back. Nothing happened that night, but fifteen days later, a perfect little finger had grown back! Signs and wonders followed the believers long after we had left Uruguay!

We were not prepared at all for what happened on the day of the Buenos Aires Healing Explosion! Before we even left the hotel, we received a call that the stadium was already packed. When we walked into the stadium, our hearts swelled with joy and humility as we realized how God can use two people who have never been to seminary or had any formal training and are just *available* to the things of God.

As we walked into the field, the crowd rose to their feet shouting, "JESUS, JESUS, JESUS!" If you've never heard that name said by fifty thousand people in unison, you have missed something so thrilling that there are absolutely no words to describe.

As we stood under a beautiful moon, we were exhilarated beyond imagination to see the power of God surge through the believers of Argentina. To see crippled bodies healed all over an audience at the same time because of a simple teaching the people have received is more than we can comprehend. How we praise God for what He is doing around the world as He prepares his body for the return of Jesus!

Chapter 18

On a Cold, Dismal Day

Before we left the hotel for our meeting in Jamestown, New York, the TV reporters were encouraging everyone to stay home because the temperature was sub-zero and roads were packed with snow which made safe travel difficult.

The evangelist always has to go, whether or not anyone else shows up. Wrapped in warm coats and scarves, we donned our snow boots and plowed through a six-foot mound of snow to get to our rental car, which was almost hidden because snow plows had really piled up some big stacks of dirty, vehicle-soiled "white stuff".

We cautiously proceeded down the slippery street to the old movie theatre where our meeting was to be held, climbed over snow mounds again, and got inside the theatre. At least, we got through the first set of entry doors. We had to wait for quite a while before anyone opened up the interior doors, and there was no heat in the foyer where we were standing, so our bodies were below normal temperature when we finally entered the building.

When we could still see our breath as we exhaled, we realized it was not a bit better inside!

I tried to find someone who worked for the theatre to tell them that the heat wasn't on, and when I finally located someone, they told us the unbelievable news that the furnace had broken and there would be no heat that afternoon!

Still wearing our coats and boots, we tried to set up our book table, but the theatre had been painted completely black, and in the area where our books were to be sold, there was just one little fifteen-watt bulb hanging down from an electric cord. We could not even see the colors on our book covers in the dim light, and we've often wondered what books the people got. It would be a miracle if they received what they asked for, because we could not read any of the titles.

Shivering and with teeth chattering, we proceeded through the next doors to look at the theatre. What a shock as we felt the dreariness of the damp, dismal auditorium! We had spoken in a lot of peculiar places, but this was the worst. The only light on the black-painted stage was again just a little fifteen-watt bulb which hung from the ceiling.

The people in Jamestown were certainly television-oriented because they listened obediently to the newscasters and stayed home in droves. Finally, somewhere between seventy-five and one hundred people found their way into the dark, uninviting building and sat there shivering and rubbing their hands together to get them warm.

It is really difficult to get into praise and worship when your teeth are coming together in a staccato beat because of the cold, but we tried a few songs anyway! During the feeble praise service, I whispered to Charles, "What are we doing here?" I was sure I had missed God because I knew He would never send us to a place like this!

One thing God has taught us over the years is to give every service "everything we've got" regardless of the size of the crowd or the circumstances. That's just what we did, even though we did dismiss the service a little quicker than normal just because we didn't want a bunch of frozen corpses out in the audience. They were all sitting there with their coats pulled up tightly around their necks; and people with physical problems don't need that kind of environment, so we started laying hands on the sick right away.

After we had laid hands on everyone there, we packed our books rapidly to take them back with us. We were the last ones to leave the theatre, and as we waded through the black snow still piled waist high in front of the theatre, we looked at each other, laughed and exclaimed, "Can anything good ever come out of Jamestown?"

About a year later, I received a copy of a newspaper from Erie, Pennsylvania, which had one of the funniest stories I had ever read, and it was written by someone who was asking the same question we did, "What are we doing here?" This is the story, which will prove beyond doubt that God can take any mess and make a miracle out of it.

Jack Grazier was a newspaper reporter for the *Erie Daily Times*. He and his wife Debbie had been attempting to have a baby for several years, but with no success. They had tried all the medical techniques, and the article said that his wife even bought him oversized boxer shorts because that was supposed to be helpful in cases like theirs.

Some friends had "drug" them to our meeting, and he wasn't impressed with anything he saw or heard. His description of me was so hysterical I won't even tell you what he said, but he described Charles as a "withered, staid looking, aging Republican!"   That didn't turn me on, but nevertheless, I continued reading the article.

This couple had never been to a charismatic service and, of course, were not prepared for what was about to happen. As people came forward and climbed up some of the most broken-down stairs I've ever seen, we began laying hands on them and they began falling under the power of God. To someone who has never seen this, it can be a tremendous shock! I remember what I thought when I went to a Kathryn Kuhlman service and saw this phenomenon for the first time. It almost blew me away because it was beyond my ability to understand how she could "do" it.

This couple was sitting out there with the same thoughts. They decided they were not going to go up onto that run-down, gloomy, depressing stage just to fall down and get their clothes dirty. Their friends kept encouraging them since they had driven so far, to at least "try" it and see what happened. So, they finally decided to come up onto the stage but vowed that they would not fall down.

The first one I came to was Debbie. When I asked her what she wanted from God, she began to cry and, through her sobs, relayed that she wanted a baby. I promptly said, "That's my specialty! I have them in all colors – red, black, white and yellow." Her husband immediately panicked because he wanted to make sure they got the right color! The reason I said this is because God has given me a very precious anointing in this area, and wherever we go, there's always a baby boom after we pray for all the couples who want babies!

I laid hands on her and said, "Father, your word says that the womb of your children will never be barren, and that you cause the barren woman to be the joyful mother of many children. I ask You to place in this womb a beautiful baby, perfect, whole and delivered within one year, in the name of Jesus!" Then, I said, as I always do, "And if it's twins, you have to name them Charles and Frances!" Then I added, my eyes meeting theirs, "Remember, every good and perfect gift comes from above."

Debbie did just what I expected her to do and what she never expected to do. She fell out under the power of God! Can you imagine the shock of her husband when he saw her lying on the floor? He looked at her and said, "You traitor!" I turned to him and asked, "What do you want Jesus to do for you?"

He muttered that he had some sort of arthritis of the chest, so I laid hands on him and commanded the spirit of arthritis to come out in the name of Jesus. He flew backward under the power of God and hit the floor with a thud, without a catcher behind him! He said the next thing he remembered was looking up at a black ceiling with a tiny little bulb hanging down, but he had absolutely no pain in his chest! They told us later that they "wobbled" off the stage in a dazed condition because they had never experienced anything like this in their entire lives.

They went home, completely baffled by the entire afternoon. How could they have fallen when Jack had braced himself against being "pushed" over? Nevertheless, it had happened, so they decided to practice at home. He got in front of the sofa, took the same stance he had taken at the theatre and said, "Go ahead, push me!" Debbie pushed with all her might, and he didn't fall down. They tried several times, but she could never push him over. They began to wonder, was there really something to this supernatural power of God?

God's word never returns void, because in April of the next year a beautiful baby boy named Ian Christian was born. Jack shared the fact that when he tells the story of how they got pregnant, people look at him and ask him if he really believes that God had anything to do with it, and he responds, "I know the mind can do strange things. Coincidences can happen. But, though it was hard at first for me to admit it, yes, I do believe that Frances Hunter and a divine power channeled through her did it!"

The thing that thrilled me so much when I read the article was, it shared about how he was standing in the birthing room, holding the baby for the first time. As Debbie beheld her husband and baby son, suddenly her eyes widened and she said, "Look at that!" as she pointed to a picture of a mother and baby on the wall directly behind him. The inscription underneath the picture read, "GOD'S GIFT!"

If the story ended right there, it would be a fabulous story, and it would have made the trip to Jamestown worthwhile, but it did not stop there. *McCall's* magazine picked up the story and printed it in the October, 1987 issue. From that, *Good Morning, New York*, the television show starring Regis Philbin, which was then watched by twelve million viewers, asked us to be guests, and we had a wonderful time sharing Jesus on the program with Jack and Debbie. Before the program, however, they both received the baptism with the Holy Spirit!

As a result of all of this, Jack was commissioned by one of the world's largest publishers to write a book on legitimate faith healers. His book, *The Power Beyond* drew accolades from both believers and skeptics. I thrilled to see the title of his first chapter, "Where Did You Come From, Baby, Dear?"

Sometimes what looks like the world's darkest situation can turn into one of the brightest. Signs and wonders will always follow you if you'll just be obedient to God and go wherever He tells you to go. This is a miracle that will never end because, even as we are drawing close to finishing this book, more miracles are in the offing because we didn't turn and run away from a miserable, damp, dark, dingy, dilapidated theatre!

Chapter 19

Heart-Warming Miracles

A Miracle "By the Book"

If you ever wondered if you could be healed even if you were not at a healing service, stop wondering, right now. God honors faith, and faith can ignite without the benefit of someone speaking to you through a microphone up on a stage. God's power can be released anywhere, anytime, even while you are reading your Bible or an anointed book.

We received the following letter which really brightened our day!

"I read your book on *How to Heal the Sick*. My daughter had been diagnosed and told to wear corrective leg braces at three weeks of age. I was to take her back in one month. I was used to this because my son also had worn braces for three years. My womb was not long enough and made their legs buckle and turn in.

"I was born again and baptized in the Holy Spirit. I got to the part in your book that said 'If you haven't tried this, do it now!'

"I was lying on the bed and my daughter was lying beside me. I stood up and reached over and laid hands on her and said, 'In Jesus' name, legs straighten.' I felt them turn and you can imagine my scream to my husband to come and see.

"I went to church and told everyone!

"Well, it came time for her check-up. I wasn't going to take her back but I knew it was good to get confirmation. The devil made it a long ten-mile trip to the doctor's office. He kept saying in my mind that she wasn't really healed. I kept saying, 'Yes, she is!' (Not knowing at that time how much authority I have in Jesus' name.)

"The doctor kept looking at his reports and x-rays and asking me her name, how to spell it, etc., etc. He was trying to assume it was not the same child. He told me it couldn't be the same legs he had x-rayed.

"My daughter is now three and has perfect legs."

A Miracle "Out of the Box"

There are not typical miracles or typical, normal or not-normal miracles. Miracles are always just the right touch from God at the point of contact when a person's faith reaches out and grabs what they desire or need.

In Tulsa, Oklahoma, which is considered the "Jerusalem" of Christianity in America, we experienced a humorous miracle. A telephone call from the person involved confirmed what others saw as they left the building.

I had prayed for a woman with diabetes who was exceptionally heavy. It is impossible to tell if someone is healed of a disease of that nature until they have been back to their doctor, so I advised her to stay on her insulin and whatever other medication she was on until she went back to her doctor for evaluation.

By the time she walked out onto the parking lot, she realized that the power of God had touched her and something was happening in her body, because her slip had "slipped" right down into soft folds around her ankles!

When she reached home, she weighed and found that she had lost twenty pounds just by God's power touching her body. Her visit back to her doctor confirmed the healing of the diabetes!

The Frozen Chosen

On a sub-zero night in Cedar Rapids, Iowa, we were just concluding our meeting when a lady approached us with an unusual prayer request. She asked us to pray for her dog which was outside in her car. Since it was bitter cold, we suggested that she go out and bring the dog in so we could lay hands on it.

She thoroughly shocked us when she answered, "Well, I can't. He died two weeks ago, and I froze him in the deep freeze, and he's in the trunk."

My mouth dropped open and I glanced at Charles, but he motioned for me to stay indoors while he followed the woman out of the building to her car. Fortunately, the building had a covered entryway and the car was just a short distance from the door. When they got there, the woman unlocked her trunk, and there lay the dog frozen stiff as a board. Charles laid hands on the dog and spoke life into it, turned around and came back into the building. That was the last evening of our meetings in Cedar Rapids, and we never did learn what became of the dog! But...you never know what is going to happen when you're in the miracle and healing ministry!

Miracle of a Heart's Desire

A miracle, sign or wonder can come in many different forms. This one happened as a result of a "specific seed" offering I had taken. I asked the audience to think of something very specific that they wanted to receive from God and to plant a seed offering to reap a harvest of the desire of their heart. God is not limited by our needs; He also delights in giving us the desires of our heart if we will only take delight in Him. Our hearts thrilled when we received a phone call followed by this letter:

"I just talked to you by phone and as promised I'm writing to tell you the exciting and wonderful things the Lord has done for me since I attended your meetings. Glory! I'm still high on God!

"On Sunday evening, you and Charles took the first offering; you said to listen to the Lord and He would tell each person the amount they should give and to be obedient without question and He would bless us.

"I had already tithed on the money I brought with me on my trip, so I had not planned to tithe, but only to give 'seed money' during my stay. But, because of what was spoken in testimonies and then in obedience to your words, I heard the still small voice of the Lord and the amount was dropped into my spirit. As the offering was held up to the Lord, you and Charles prayed.

"You asked the Lord to bless each person and that whatever each person had asked for, that you and Charles would stand in agreement and then (here's where it gets good!) you said, '...Charles and I believe that God will not only bless your giving but He will do it before November 30!'

"As you prayed, I lifted my gift to the Lord and said, 'Father God, I want to find my sister by my mom's birthday, November 23rd and Lord, I thank you right now that you are doing it. Amen.'

"I had been searching for my sister, Terry Jean, for many, many years. We were separated as infants by adoption and I only had a picture of her at the age of two years.

"God worked many miracles! God moves quickly! In less than two and one-half weeks I talked to my sister, Terry Jean, for the first time in thirty-four years. On my mom's birthday I met Terry Jean at the Kansas City airport and we embraced for the first time in thirty-four years. The joy of this hour is not expressible in words.

"You've helped to teach me to listen and be obedient in my giving and for that, may our Lord bless you both a thousand-fold return on ALL your giving.

"Much love, joy and peace in Christ,"   D.L.C.

Miracle Honeymoon

Marriages can be healed through a sign and a

wonder. This one happened on a cold, snowy night in Minneapolis, Minnesota.

The Holy Spirit brought to our attention that there were a lot of people who needed to be delivered of cigarettes, so we had what we call a "cigarette stomp." This is a really decisive action where we let the people who want to be set free from the bondage of tobacco get their packs of cigarettes out of their coats or purses, throw them to the floor and "stomp" on them!

Two people came from opposite sides of the stage, and met each other standing in line. None of us knew their story until later, but they had filed papers for divorce because their marriage was at an end. They said nothing to each other while they were waiting in line.

When we laid hands on the woman, she fell under the power of God. The man was next. We laid hands on him and he dropped to the floor under the power.

She was still on the floor when he jumped up, took one look at her and exclaimed, "I've got a new wife!"

She opened her eyes, gazed up at him and said, "I've got a new husband!"

He didn't even give her time to go back to the stands to get her coat. He picked her up in his arms and ran out of Augsburg College yelling, "We're going on a honeymoon!"

God truly hates divorce, and I can imagine heaven rejoicing as this couple began a brand new life together.

Chapter 20

Arriving With Gifts

Never have I been touched by any human interest story as much as I was touched in the Philippines. Some people have a tremendous hunger for God and are willing to do anything and everything to satisfy that hunger or to seek a closer walk with God.

The pastor of a church in Mindanao received a letter from a friend in California encouraging him and his wife to come to the Healing Explosion in Manila. To go by plane was very expensive, and their only other choice was a two-day and two-night trip by boat.

Much of the Philippines is poverty-stricken, and most people simply do not have the finances to do the things they would like to do. This couple's church building had been destroyed by a typhoon two years before. They rebuilt it, and the next year it was again destroyed by a typhoon. They were faced with rebuilding their church for the second time in two years. Their hearts were deeply stirred when they heard about the new wave of healing revival and what God is doing in the world. They purposed in their hearts that somehow or other they were going to get to the Healing Explosion and take the message back to their island and their people.

The pastor and his wife went to a pawn shop and mortgaged several things which they felt they could do without. The money they received was not enough.

They returned to the shop with their wristwatches, even though time is an important thing in the world today. What they received was still not enough to make the trip.

They returned home and gathered up everything that had any value at all, mortgaged it at the pawn shop, and they still did not have the amount of money they needed.

Then they turned to the last thing they had left. They examined their food supply for the next year. In the Philippines, many people raise their own chickens and pigs, and they had three piglets which would provide them with an ample supply of meat when they were grown. They took the piglets to market and sold them.

When they put all the money together from mortgaging all their personal belongings, including the year's supply of meat for their table, they had $40.00, which was just enough to pay their fare one way on the boat. They boarded rejoicing, with not an ounce of regret for any of their sacrifice.

Full of faith and hope, they came to Manila. They believed God had special revelation for them, and they couldn't wait to see what He was doing in the world and what He wanted for the island of

Mindanao.

They arrived with gifts, however. They brought us some beautiful dried mangos which were absolutely delicious. They wanted to give, even though they really needed to receive. But then, that is the principle of God, isn't it?

We did not hear the story until the second day. We did not know that they didn't even have cab fare, which is minimal in the Philippines where you can go anywhere for fifty cents. They would not even have gotten to the meeting the first night, except that someone heard of their plight and paid their cab fare for them. Then, God spoke to someone else to provide them with housing and food for their stay!

Our hearts were so stirred that we took an offering for them from the American healing teams and raised 7,000 pesos, which was then about $350.00. How they rejoiced over what God had done!

As we observed this precious couple and their hunger for the things of God, all Charles and I could think about was, "How many of us would be willing to mortgage all our earthly possessions so we could go to a meeting to find out God's message for the hour and take it back to our people?"

Chapter 21

It's Happening Today

All of the fabulous miracles which are chronicled in this book have been followed by a consistent flow of praise reports. We want to share a few of the most exciting testimonies we have received over the last year, and in particular some of those which have come in just during the last few weeks!

Around the World

We sensed the excitement of a shepherd in Brazil who wrote in broken English that he has been ministering to the sick and seeing miracles after watching *How to Heal the Sick.* A lady in the Philippines received a brand new liver from God after a believer laid hands on her. Doctors were flabbergasted when a glaucoma patient had normal pressure tests after a church member laid hands on her. A boy who could not walk or speak plainly was walking, running and speaking clearly after a healing service in a believer's home. Someone had tumors disappear from their body, verified by medical tests which all came back negative. And little babies of all colors are being born supernaturally all over the place!

Healing schools and healing explosions are taking place somewhere even as this page is being written. We can hardly wait to get to the office each morning to see what God has done while we were sleeping!

Some of the testimonies we receive are a result of prayers by Charles and me, some are a result of faith released through anointed prayer cloths (and even "electronic" prayer cloths), others are a result of someone learning their authority in Jesus' name through our meetings, books, videotapes or DVDs. What is especially thrilling is that ordinary believers are leading people to Jesus, getting them baptized with the Holy Spirit, casting out devils and laying hands on the sick with signs and wonders following.

This e-mail just came in, and we rejoiced to note the sincere detail with which this pastor ministered. He had come all the way from Nigeria to be ordained in our March, 2008 Ordination service and returned to lay hands on the sick. In the pastor's words,

"The young man had been diagnosed with compression of the waist bones, which is a painful condition making it very difficult to sit down. He was a driver, and being unable to sit, his job was in jeopardy. Orthopedic doctors had examined him and said he needed an operation which would cost half a million Nigerian Naira. His family was trying desperately to raise money for the operation when they brought him to the healing service.

"I had to apply 'the pelvic thing' on him and held his two toes of his legs and allowed the healing anointing to flow through his legs to his hip.

"After that, he got up healed by the power of the Holy Ghost in the name of Jesus. The devil is defeated. When I asked him to sit earlier, he was in terrible pain, but after the pelvic thing, he jumped and sat and walked and sat freely without pain. The church erupted in praise and dance as we gave Jesus Christ the glory!"

From Australia came this exciting letter:

"Hi, I am the wife of the pastor in a small church in southwestern Victoria, Australia. I recently purchased a 7-hour training pack after reading *How to Heal the Sick*. I planned to use it to train up my ladies group (all 6 of us) to minister healing to our church. I thought you might like to hear what happened after watching the third session yesterday.

"Half way through the DVD, Charles invites those in the audience to stand and do the growing out of arms thing. We all stood to participate as well. As we found out later, there were a few skeptics among us, but God proved himself faithful regardless.

"One lady had come with severe backache and muscle pain from long hours of standing. She nearly didn't come to the meeting because of the pain. Well, Charles started to go through the procedure and all of a sudden this dear lady is starting to cry. Another lady sitting beside her starts to make the commands just as Charles directed.

"Not only was this beautiful lady set free from back pain completely but she was also set free from some demonic presence that refused to allow her to thank Jesus. Praise, God He is awesome.

"Then, it was on for young and old; each of us had some need for healing and it was just as if the floodgates opened. All of us were touched in some way, and what is usually a 1-2 hour morning meeting went on for over four hours as healings turned to praise and worship of our great God.

"We will finish watching the rest of the DVD next week (it kind of got forgotten in the excitement). None of us can wait to see what will happen next. I would have loved to be a fly on the wall in some of their homes last night as they shared what an amazing day we had and how wonderful our God is. So thank you, thank you, thank you. May God bless your ministry even more abundantly."

Still Praising God

This letter came in just recently from someone whose rather unique miracle so dramatically impacted her life that, over thirty years later, she was prompted to share it with us:

"I am not sure of the exact date, but, it was probably in the 70's...I was getting ready to go to marriage counseling. The TV was on a Christian show and the host was speaking to the Happy Hunters. Frances was talking about inner healing and stopped suddenly and announced, 'We need to pray for people for inner healing.'

"I sat in front of the TV as Frances began praying. All I heard was, 'and if you were not wanted as a child...'

"I covered my eyes tightly and began sobbing. I felt the pressure of Jesus' hand on my head, and was aware of light even with my eyes closed. That moment is as real today as it was then. Only now I appreciate it so much more. The thought then came to me that I probably wasn't wanted as a child (third girl!) but I knew I was wanted now!

"At a later time it was confirmed by my mother... and she apologized. That prayer changed my life. That encounter with the Lord remains deeply in my heart and I treasure that more than anything else in my life. Thank you for your ministry. My friend went to a recent class and was excited about the Hunters and told me to look up your website. I am thrilled to see you are still sharing and blessing people."

Snakebite Disappears

Just a few days ago, a 72-year old grandmother in Texas was bitten by a copperhead snake. The hospital wanted to keep her overnight and give her medication, but her husband was ill, and she wanted to be at home where she could care for him. She drove home, and she and her husband laid hands on the red, swollen wound and commanded it to be healed. The next morning, there was no evidence of the wound!

Miracles Every Day!

You can hardly get more current than while the final proofing of a book is being done. We had two miracles in two days which were connected to people right in our office!

A young man who has been on our staff for several years has a 13-year-old nephew who left this week for an Eagle Scout camping trip. The location was miles out in the wilderness, so far removed from civilization that, when you got to the end of the paved road, the camp was still seven miles beyond.

As the campers were settling in, the young scout had a violent asthma attack. He stopped breathing three times and fell to his knees, gasping for breath. A woman told him later that she could see the devil just sucking his breath out of him, trying to take his life.

When the owner of the camp had left the group, he had said, "Let me give you my cell phone number in the event you need any help." The Christian scout leader knew that cell phones would not work in that remote area, but entered the owner's number into his phone anyway. As soon as the young boy had the asthma attack, he dialed the man's number and it worked! He explained briefly what had happened and told him to call "911" and get an ambulance there at once. After making the call, all he knew to do was pray.

The speeding ambulance could go only so far before the paved road abruptly ended, and then they continued as far as they could on a narrow, unsurfaced road. Unable to proceed further in the vehicle, the crew unloaded an oxygen tank, emergency medical supplies and a gurney, and carried everything for two miles to get to the boy. When the scout was moved onto the gurney, he refused to lie down.   Everyone said, "Lay him down!   Lay him down!"   But the scout leader directed, "No, let him stay in the position he is in." Doctors later reported that if they had laid him down, he would have died.

What could have turned out as a tragic report on the evening news became a time of rejoicing. People were praising God all over the place, because God had allowed a cell phone to work which was too far from any towers to pick up signals, and the Holy Spirit was directing all along that the boy should not lie down.   He is alive and well and, as you can imagine, our entire office is rejoicing!

Charles and I hate to ever end a book because we know that the minute we send it to the printer, something else exciting is going to happen that we would have wanted to include!   This next miracle is one of those exhilarating ones that actually happened just in time to add it to this chapter!

We got an alarming phone call in our office. A friend of ours was watching her 3-year-old grandson because her daughter had just given birth to a baby girl.   When it was time for them to be released, she had to go to the hospital to help her daughter pack to come home.

Since she knew her hands would really be full in helping her daughter and new baby get home, she took her little grandson to a professional baby sitter and then started out for the hospital.   As she was driving, she received a frantic call from the babysitter.

The babysitter screamed, "Your grandson has just drowned!"

One minute he had been right before her eyes in a little baby float, the next minute he was floating face down on the water. The woman came totally unglued. She managed to lift his limp body out of the water and wrap him in a towel, but she had not even called "911" yet and was sobbing hysterically into the phone, "What shall I do?"

Our friend dialed "911" as she made a U-Turn and sped back to the house where she had left her grandson. Just before she arrived at the home, her heart jumped into her throat as she saw the ambulance already speeding away with the toddler. She raced madly behind the light-flashing, siren-screaming ambulance to the hospital emergency room.

While she was frantically driving behind the ambulance, she called one of the girls in our office, who immediately called me. We commanded the spirit of death to come out of the child in the name of Jesus; we commanded the brain to be normal and all the organs to work properly; we commanded the spirit of life to come back into him in Jesus' name.

The emergency team was able to revive the child so that he was breathing. However the CAT scan they performed revealed that his brain was swelling. When the brain is swelling, that means "Danger, Danger, Danger!" The situation looked grim.

The boy's grandmother called us again. We immediately commanded a new brain to form in that baby in Jesus' name. Back at the hospital, the medical team put him into an induced coma and waited. We continued thanking Jesus for a brand new brain.

Two days later, (today!) we received the exciting news that a new brain scan had been done which showed absolutely no swelling and the brain was completely normal. As his grandmother spoke with us, he was sitting up in his bed eating a popsicle!

Miracles Any Place

God does incredible miracles every day. This is an "old" miracle, and yet no miracle ever becomes old; it is always new because, when you see someone whose life has been completely restored to them, it is an occasion for continual rejoicing. We are including this miracle in our final chapter because we see this couple on a regular basis, and our hearts continue to overflow with joy every time we see them.

A pastor of a large church in Colorado was devastated when his wife was diagnosed with lupus, in the prime of her life. Her case was so serious that doctors told her she had three years, maximum, to live and advised him to give up his church and spend quality time with his wife.

They left their church and relocated to California, where she spent 14 months lying in bed in a hotel. Her condition only deteriorated and, as she realized the doctor's prediction was closing in, she said to her husband, "If I have just this little while to live, I want to be near my grandkids and my daughter." Her grandchildren and daughter happened to live in Kingwood, Texas.

Her husband promptly responded, "OK, sweetheart, we're moving there right now." They packed all their belongings, moved to Kingwood and, as God would have it, they took over a small church just a short distance down the street from where our ministry offices were located.

Both the pastor and his wife had heard about "The Happy Hunters" and, although the pastor later confided that we "scared" him, he wanted us to pray for his wife. When he called the office, our secretary told him that we had a white Lincoln with a navy blue top, and whenever he saw the car outside, to stop and come in. However, it seemed that every time he drove by our office, our car was not there because we out of town.

One Sunday night, after church, we were sitting in the parking lot of a large grocery store in our area. Charles had gone into the store, and I had remained in the car along with Dr. and Mrs. Roy LeRoy. Suddenly, a man walked up, tapped on the window and asked, "Are you Frances Hunter?"

I rolled down the window and answered, "Yes."

He told me the story about his wife having lupus, and I immediately asked, "Where is she?" All I could think about was, "Let's get out of this car and let's go and pray for her!" But he smiled and responded, "No, I'll bring her over here."

He went over to their car, but his wife didn't want to get out because of the visible effects of lupus. She had lost her hair, and white hair resembling that of a wolf (which is what the word "lupus" means) was growing on her hands and her face. She was very self-conscious about her appearance and did not want anyone to see her. However, he insisted, and they came over to where we waited inside our car, in the grocery store parking lot.

Dr. LeRoy and I both laid hands on her and commanded the spirit of lupus to come out in Jesus' name! We commanded every cancer cell in her body to die, including the root and seed of every cancer cell, in the name of Jesus; and we spoke life into her and commanded all traces of lupus to go!

This happened eight years ago, and this woman was wonderfully healed and remains in perfect health today. After five years, she was declared to not be in remission but totally healed, and her health insurance was completely restored in full. Her beautiful hair and complexion returned completely, and her entire countenance continues to radiate the glory of God! Praise God for what He does yesterday, today and forever!

Epilogue

Let's Get the Job Done for Jesus!

Charles and I pray that, throughout this book, you have been able to experience the tremendous move of God through hundreds of thousands of people coming to Healing Explosions, churches, school auditoriums and even private homes, expecting to receive the supernatural. The thing that we want to burn deep into your souls is that the multitudes being saved and receiving the baptism with the Holy Spirit, the exciting healings and supernatural miracles, happened not just through the ministry of two people but through thousands of ordinary believers from all walks of life, all colors, all nations – who accepted their responsibility to do the Great Commission.

The great healing schools and Healing Explosions you read about were simply training grounds and launching pads to get all believers confident that they can do the works that Jesus did and greater works. The entire thrust of our ministry has been, don't depend on Charles and Frances, don't just watch someone up on a stage somewhere, because "If Charles and Frances can do it, you can do it, too!"

We want each and every one who reads this book to see yourself doing the same things others are doing who have learned how to release the mighty power of God. People that you come in contact with every day need to learn about a living, miracle-working Jesus and how He can work through every believer. The book of Acts is still being written! Let's ALL be a part of it!

Start a Bible Healing School!

Start a Bible Healing School right now because you can change your own life, plus the life of every person around you, your church, your neighborhood, your city.

It is easy to start a healing school!

All you need to start a healing school is our 7 hour Power Pack DVD which shows you how to heal the sick and two books, How To Heal The Sick and Handbook For Healing.

The first thing you need to do is be excited.

If you have not been to a healing school, watch the DVD's first and you will be super excited about sharing this information with other people.

Decide on which night of the week or which day of the week you want to have your meeting and you can show either one or two hours each night.

After showing the Bible healing schools then you have everybody lay hands on the sick.

It is amazing what will happen to the enthusiasm of everybody and what will happen to you.

The first part of the tape is called, "Miracles, Miracles, Miracles." It is so vital to show this first so people can actually see miracles happening today.

There is not a day goes by in our office where we don't get telephone calls from people that we have prayed for over the telephone or prayed for in person and who are healed.

Call our office at (281) 358-7575 or look at our website at www.cfhunter.org and see the different healing packages you can use, then get your credit card and call our office and we will ship all the materials you need the same day or the next day. See the packages listed on the next page and call for special prices.

You might say, "Who am I going to invite?" The first time invite your friends, your neighbors, and if necessary or if you are in a church, invite some members of your church.

Don't stop at just one healing school, continue them on because you will be amazed what they will do for you and what they will do for other people.

DIAMOND PACKAGES

Call our office for special prices!

BLUE Diamond Pack (Order #2005)

Books: How To Heal The Sick · Handbook For Healing · How To Receive and Maintain a Healing · The Supernatural Spine · God's Healing Promises · Healing Through Humor · How To Heal The Sick 15-Hour Study Guide · Power Pack Study Guide · Joan Hunter's Healing the Whole Man Handbook

DVDs: How To Heal The Sick (15 Hours) · Power Pack (7 Hours) · New Ways To Heal The Sick (1 Hour) · Advanced Teaching - How To Heal The Sick (12 Hours) · Lakeland Healing Explosion (12 Hours) · Doctor's Panel (6 Hours)

CDs: 7 Steps To Minister Healing Successfully · Healing Is For You · Crash Course in Evangelism · Which One Are You? · How To Reach The World For Jesus

WHITE Diamond Pack (Order #2006)

Books: How To Heal The Sick · Handbook For Healing · How To Receive and Maintain a Healing · The Supernatural Spine · How To Heal The Sick Study Guide · Power Pack Study Guide

DVDs: How To Heal The Sick (15 Hours) · Power Pack (7 Hours)

CDs: New Ways To Heal The Sick · 7 Steps To Minister Healing Successfully · Healing Is For You

PINK Diamond Pack (Order #2007)

Books: How To Heal The Sick · Handbook For Healing · How To Receive and Maintain a Healing · The Supernatural Spine · How To Heal The Sick Study Guide

DVDs: How To Heal The Sick (15 Hours)

CDs: 7 Steps To Minister Healing Successfully · Healing Is For You

YELLOW Diamond Pack (Order #2008)

Books: How To Heal The Sick · Handbook For Healing · How To Receive and Maintain a Healing · The Supernatural Spine · God's Healing Promises · Power Pack Study Guide

DVDs: Power Pack (7 Hours)

CD: Healing Is For You

Vision

Equipping Believers to take the healing power of God beyond the 4 walls of the church and to the 4 corners of the earth.

♥ To AWAKEN the Body of Christ with the vision that they can and must do the same things that Jesus did.

♥ To INFORM the Body of Christ that laying hands on the sick is not an option, but a mandate from Jesus to all believers.

♥ To TRAIN those who desire to know more.

♥ To RESTORE the hearts of men to God and confirm their value to Him.

♥ To IMPART the anointing and the giftings of God to all that want them.

♥ To REACH the lost by demonstrating God's power and sharing His love.

♥ To OPEN their eyes to the purpose and callings that God has for them.

The vision of Hunter Ministries and Joan Hunter Ministries is to see people all over the world healed and set free: spiritually, physically, mentally, emotionally and financially.

HUNTER MINISTRIES
P. O. Box 5600 • Kingwood TX 77325
(281) 358-7575 • (281) 358-4130 Fax
Website: www.cfhunter.org
eMail: wec@cfhunter.org